THE
JOAN CHRONICLES

Pearls of Wisdom on the Journey to Heaven

Sara Pizano, MA, DVM

AuthorHouse™
1663 Liberty Drive
Bloomington, IN 47403
www.authorhouse.com
Phone: 1-800-839-8640

Published by AuthorHouse   03/26/2015

ISBN: 978-1-4969-1489-7 (sc)
ISBN: 978-1-4969-1488-0 (e)

Library of Congress Control Number: 2014914182

Print information available on the last page.

This book is printed on acid-free paper.

CONTENTS

This book is dedicated to my mom.

ACKNOWLEDGEMENTS

Many thanks go out to all the people who loved my mom and whom she loved back. I call them The Collection. They are family and friends with little distinction between the two categories. They are a collection of people through the years that stayed connected through time and across many miles. To all of you, I give my heartfelt and grateful appreciation. Your love lifted my mom to unimaginable heights and your encouragement during this journey and through the publishing of this story has meant the world to me.

Thank you to my awesome editor, Judith Faerron and to my friends who took the time to thoughtfully review the manuscript, Andrea "AJ" Catalano, Yvonne Grassie, Barbara Pinto, Ilidia Alvarez-Landestoy and Ericka Cohen.

Thank you to Lexi Levere, Coley Levere and Isabelle Pluchino for being the perfect fill-in grandchildren and far wiser than their few years.

May we all live and finish as well as my mom.

PREFACE

Joan Rita Hahn was born on November 24, 1936, in the small town of Minersville, Pennsylvania. The main industry in Minersville was—you guessed it—coal mining, but our main family business was funerals.

My mom grew up with her extended family in a large funeral home, and she kept amazing memories of that innocent time. Like most girls, she had two life goals: to have a family and a home of her own.

After high school she received a degree from the Reading School of Nursing, because she believed it would enable her to be a "better mom" to her future children.

And an amazing mom she was. With my dad's encouragement, she chose to stay home and make sure my brother, Rafael, and I had a hot breakfast and a healthy dinner. In 1971, our family purchased a home with seven bedrooms overlooking endless acres. We never did without, and it was many decades before I understood and truly appreciated that this was solely because of mom's incredible money managing skills and, as one friend put it, her ability to "stretch a dollar like nobody's business."

And so it was, in February 2012, when her oncology team said they had no further treatment options following her two-year battle with ovarian cancer, that I left my home in Florida and moved back to the house where I grew up in order to care for my mom. Thanks to my medical training as a veterinarian, I was able to manage her hospice care and doctors' orders at home—with IV fluids, medications and an intravenous morphine pump—so she would not have to be hospitalized. Friends called it "amazing" and "difficult," but I saw it as one of God's greatest blessings in my life, and a true honor. An opportunity to help her finish well.

During one of her last hospital stays it became too emotionally difficult to call the many friends and family who cared so much about her, so I started sending out daily group email updates. Years before, her friend Kevin had nicknamed her "The Joan," because her personality was just too big to have a single first name—like Donald Trump being called "The Donald."

So my updates came to be known as The Joan Chronicles, or TJC, and they helped our loved ones deal with the inevitable. Those loved ones forwarded them on to friends going through similar trials, and there was a great ripple effect. To this day I don't know exactly how many people followed our journey during that time, but even those who never met my mom fell in love with her through TJC, and shared in our triumphs and trials.

In the depths of great and ongoing physical pain, my mom never complained, she was never angry and I don't believe she ever cried about her illness. She likened the suffering to childbirth. You experience unbearable pain giving birth but you know that on the other side of it is the indescribable miracle of a baby. My mom felt that the pain she suffered with during her illness would only lead her to the indescribable miracle of Heaven. It was very simple.

Friends and family sent endless cards, emails and well wishes, really too many to count and most so touching that it was hard to believe that one person could absorb so much love. My mom seemed to have an endless capacity to give and receive, and I realized that through TJC our loved ones comforted me as much as I comforted them.

Dear Sara,

Thank you so very, very much for writing such witty, informative, make-the-best-of-things updates about your precious, wonderful, loving, lovable mother—updates that carry the essence of the adorable, delightful, magical, fabulous The Joan we all fell madly in love with the minute we met her, and who we came to love even more dearly and deeply as we got to know her. My memories of our days together in Japan are some of the most treasured ones I have....

* * *

Dear Joanie,

Thank you for all the good times and memories you gave me growing up and for all the times you "cured" me for my mother. I know she would not have been able to survive us kids without you. From broken legs to poison ivy, you were our savior! Your "pearls" will/do ring in our heads forever. Every time the weather changes, hot, cold, or rainy, I hear, "You really should keep your head covered." You have given my girls so many joyous times, good advice, taught them many things and have given them so many wonderful memories. Our lives were blessed to have you in our "family."

* * *

Dear Sara,

Joanie has such amazing courage and faith, as well as strength to go through everything.... I am in awe of her grace. I am filling up with tears as I write these words to you, I have come to know and be so fond of all of you. I am having overwhelming feelings of happiness and sadness all at the same time. Sending you all my heartfelt love and prayers for ease and peace in these coming days....

* * *

Dear Joan,

Even though we didn't get to see each other much over the years, I hope you know how special you have always been to me. You were such a blessing to me as a young mother when I lived in NY, and so clueless about so many things. Such a great person to know and friend to treasure. Please know I'm praying for you and your family for God's healing touch and peace and comfort.

* * *

Dear Sara,

No one was a stranger to your mom, just a friend she hadn't met yet. I knew it from all the stories my mom shared with me and I felt grateful to have experienced it for a few years in person. Please give her a kiss from me. She is an amazing woman. Both of your parents are people who embed themselves deep in the hearts of those who get to know them. Share with her that I send my love and prayers. If she's up for a hug, give her one of those too and let her know I love when she chooses the light green, she looks great in that shade....

* * *

Evenin' Little Joanie,

Our stay at 107 Columbia Hill yesterday was a charming visit, one we will treasure for a lifetime. While departing 107 Main, we commented on the charm and warmth that radiated from that little cottage, obviously the warmth we felt came from the loving people living down in that "third house on the left." We enjoyed the view and delightful meal but really need to know how you arranged for us to eat along with the deer! ...

* * *

Dear Sara,

Monica and I would like to thank you for keeping us in the loop on The Joan's condition. As we read your communiqués, we realize that you are drawing prose pictures of The Joan's character, personality and indomitable spirit. In short, you are telling us what a wonderful, courageous person your mother is. Joanie is soldiering on despite severe pain and nausea. Even with the ravages of her illness, she is trying to maintain the cheerful outlook for which she is famous.

It is a privilege to know her and her wonderful family who have rallied around her during these trying times. May we all meet in the future under happier circumstances. We send good thoughts and best wishes to The Joan and all of you....

* * *

Dear Joan,

No matter how things have gone, I want to let you know how truly blessed I have felt to have you in my life. You and Serge have been a part of it before I was born and no matter what, in my heart of hearts, you both will be a part of it, continuing the positive influences long after we've all passed on to the other side. I was honored to share life with *you as part of your family for some years, and I'll be forever grateful. You introduced me to the ashram, mocha ice cream, Breugel and how to grow successful peonies (away from the house because of the ants). You are an impeccable example of how to live, be kind, and seek balance. Because of you, I believe in winter and that balance can be found at the bottom of a bowl of borscht with sour cream and good company!*

Anyway, there's too much to put in here and I promised brevity. So I'll sum it up by reminding you that though our paths diverged, my love and gratitude for you in the world and in my life has never, not once, wavered or frayed. You are an incredible woman, mother, friend. I love you Joan and I don't intend to stop....

* * *

Dear Sara,

I am grateful for all the times Joanie visited Minersville when I was there. It was always something to look forward to and always an experience when "Joanie came home." I always had to behave myself!...

* * *

Dear Sara,

I'm sure you know how precious your mom is and how I feel so lucky to have her as my aunt. She was my lifeline when I was at first dealing with my mom's condition and Nana. Do you know she actually told me she was sorry when she told me she had cancer? I've always looked up to her and I wish I was more like her. Please, please tell me if there's anything at all I can do. I can be there in 3 hours....

* * *

Dear Sara,

I am so privileged to have met your Nana, Joanie and now you, Sara. Three generations of amazing women, very much alike in so many ways and yet so different. But at the core one common thing in all three of you is your LOVE and your incredible generous and giving nature. You are a gift to the world and all you touch. Yes, my sense is that your Nana is watching and guiding you all the different ways. What an incredible year this has been with so much pain and frustration yet so much joy and so much Grace!...

* * *

There are many words to describe my mom, but those spoken at the Celebration of her Life on August 2, 2012 capture the essence of Joan Rita Hahn Pizano like few others. As her godson, Thierry, put it:

"It didn't matter how old or young we were—for all my life, there was a constant about Aunt Joanie—you knew there was a solution if you wanted it, a suggestion shared, some hint for good health.... These are just words, but... the effect of Aunt Joan... on our lives has been more impactful than any other of our actual blood relatives. How did this happen? I don't know... but something about [her] would make you want to share every dream, every success, every heartbreak, every story....

I don't recall Aunt Joan ever asking for anything; but she was always giving.... Perhaps that's why she had so many friends—in the States and abroad. She had this rare gift in which you just wanted to be around her....

How very lucky we are that she was a part of our lives; how very special we were to have been blessed by her impact; how fortunate we were that she touched us in so many ways."

Those may be just words, but truer words were never spoken. Joanie's lifelong friends near and far would undoubtedly agree with Susan Kantor, who said:

"Joan was a friend like no one else... the most compassionate, honest, sympathetic and nonjudgmental person there could be. Joan was always there for whoever needed her...."

This is my mom's story; a story about someone completely unafraid to die, and who knew for sure she was going to Heaven. My mom was never "dying of cancer"—she *lived* until her last breath.

Her life and passing offer a lesson—a "Pearl" if you will—that every one of us needs to learn.

CHAPTER 1

There is a saying that goes like this: "It's amazing how wise our parents become as we get older." We all go through stages in life when our perceptions of our parents evolve from heroes to annoyances and back to heroes. I guess it's God's way of maturing us. We need to be separated in our teens and grow on our own for a while before returning to the nest by choice. I can see that progression in my own life, but it wasn't until the year my mom passed to Heaven that her truly awesome spirit—and how deeply she was connected to so many—became evident to me.

If you are inclined to debate nature versus nurture, Joan Rita and her older sister, Mary Jane, would be an excellent case study. Joan remembers a happy childhood filled with the fellowship of her extended family, fond memories of her grandmother's favorite recipes, the family farm, and nothing but happy times.

From left to right: Sister Jane, Brother George and Joan, late 1930s

If Mary Jane remembered anything (she constantly swore my mom was "making stuff up" about their childhood) it was usually negative. Joan put on her rose-colored glasses at an early age and chose to live the life of an eternal optimist.

Still, she was close to Jane—the ravishing beauty/Natalie Wood lookalike who said whatever was on her mind, politically correct or not.

Sisters Jane and Joan, 1950

Joan was the petite, prim and proper girl who wore gloves and hats to church without fail. Even into her seventies, repeating "The First Bra Story" made Joan cringe:

Jane was assigned to accompany Joan to the department store to purchase her first brassiere. There she announced to the saleslady that she thought there was no need for a bra—a couple of Band-Aids over Joan's nipples would suffice. My mom remained mortified and emotionally scarred for life because of that comment!

My Aunt Jane settled in Minersville after she married a mortician—go figure. It's in the family blood, so to speak, which I acknowledge is a creepy thought. My great-grandfather, grandfather, great-uncle and uncle were all Minersville morticians. Jane's son, Mark, also became a mortician (take note, this is a foretoken). I guess someone has to do it.

My Nana once commented to me that nobody had died recently in Minersville. "That's good," I said, and she responded: "Yes, but funeral directors need to live!" It's all about perspective, I guess.

In retrospect, I can see how Adams Family-esque this may sound, but growing up around dead people was totally normal for us. My Aunt Jane and Uncle Joe lived in their own funeral home as well.

The family funeral home

My aunt's job was applying make-up and doing the hair of the "dearly departed." During my school vacations in Minersville, I would often play on the floor of the viewing room or keep my aunt company during these makeovers. That viewing room, by the way, was the same room set up for family celebrations at Thanksgiving and Christmas (don't worry, any and all bodies were wheeled back into the morgue for safekeeping and sanitary eating).

So, being around dead bodies didn't faze us at all—but I can tell you now, it's a different story when it's someone you love. A certain level of ease around dead people does not prepare you emotionally for losing a loved one or seeing their physical shell. And, with no disrespect to my ancestors and heritage, I still can't get over the fact that we pump our loved ones' bodies with formaldehyde, dress them up, and bury them in very pricey non-biodegradable boxes. I personally want to be cremated and fertilize something, for God's sake! But I digress—this is about Joanie, not my end-of-life wishes.

Joan was the family renegade and the only one to leave Minersville for good. She felt called to attend nursing school and moved to the big city—Reading, Pennsylvania.

Joan's Nursing School Graduation picture, 1957

While her motivation was to be a better mother to her future children, her education led to an opportunity to work in a New York City public health center and then Columbia Presbyterian Hospital.

That's when she accidentally went on a date with my future father.

Sergio Rafael Pizano was born in Manhattan to a Columbian father and Costa Rican mother.

Serge with his parents, Clementina and Felix, mid 1930s

He didn't speak English until he was five, and—interestingly enough—later taught English and Spanish as a college professor. Serge was a City Boy, and in 1959 worked as a night admissions clerk at Columbia Presbyterian, where my mom was a nurse.

One night my Mom was preparing to go to Minersville for the Christmas holidays and—being a true organizer and anti-procrastinator—had laid out her clothes, including little nighties, on her bed. Unbeknownst to my mom, her roommate and fellow nurse Alice, and her boyfriend, Morty, were going to a German restaurant called The Heidelberg, on Second Avenue (*still* operating to this day!), and dragged Morty's childhood friend Serge with them.

Serge and Morty showed up at the apartment in the middle of Joanie's holiday packing preparations and Serge decided to enter the Forbidden Zone—Joan's bedroom (GASP!!!)—to convince her to join them as his default date. She politely declined and was highly unimpressed that Serge should enter a single lady's bedroom—uninvited, no less! *You're not in Minersville anymore, Dorothy!*

But, as luck would have it, Serge charmed her into it and off the four of them went on Christmas Eve, with Joan and Serge stuffed into the tiny backseat of Morty's Morgan. Now here is the part of the story where I cannot say with certainty what happened next, as there are varying eyewitness accounts. My mom says she was kidding around and threw a ball of pristine snow at my dad. My dad says the snowball was laced with city dirt and dog urine and alas, she had good aim. Entering the restaurant, Morty whispered, "Serge...watch out for that one...you're going to marry her." Serge and Morty do agree on that piece of historical data.

My parents were married on August 19, 1961, and my dad never got over the fact that the sweet little Minersville Catholic Church would not let nice Jewish Morty Goldstein from Manhattan stand as his best man. (This is another foretoken—you will have to wait until the end for the redemption story—I will be sure to point it out.)

Wedding day

But married they were, and a year later my brother Rafael was born. Since his name takes too long to say, everyone just calls him "Ra." I arrived two years later, to my brother's great dismay. I heard that once he was quite bored holding baby me and was going to toss me on the floor. My mom claimed she caught me before I met the tile but I do have occasional yet unexplained headaches to this day.

My brother Rafael helping me with my shoes, 1965

When I was a year old we moved to Fair Haven, Vermont. This was quite the transition for my dad—born and bred in New York City—but as much as my mom loved the excitement, she didn't want to raise her children in the Concrete Jungle.

Vermont in 1965... *hmmmm*... In an attempt to remain politically correct and on task I will offer just a hint as to the predominant population: WASP. I point this out not to insinuate this is a bad thing, but the locals did live a sheltered life with exposure to a very limited ethnic population—theirs. That means no Hispanics, black people or last names ending with "stein" or "berg."

During the summer some thought my Hispanic dad was African American because he developed such a deep tan, and they did not know what to make of him. He dared not utter a word in his native Spanish, so the only words my brother and I mastered as children were "Noche" (our dog's name) and "Dia" (our cat's name). Not only that, we pronounced Noche: *Nooo-chee.*

We were hopelessly unilingual and this would plague my mom her entire life. She could never accept that my dad didn't speak to us in

Spanish when we were little so we would grow up bilingual. But my poor father felt like a Hispanic fish out of water, so stuck to the English-only theme. Thank God she is finally at peace in Heaven, but I am now considering purchasing Rosetta Stone to become fluent in her honor, after several failed attempts throughout my life.

Noche, our Border Collie mix, is a whole other book. Our family adopted her when I was a year old and she was my best friend. It was because of my deep bond with her that I chose my future career. When I was three years old, I announced to my parents that I would be a "vegetarian."

Noche and me, 1966

Initially confused that their toddler might already be making independent philosophical choices, they finally deduced that I meant "vet-er-i-nar-ian." So while other children switched career dreams on a whim, I was steadfast. I never changed my mind. It was my normal—like being around dead people on summer vacation.

In college, I was totally shocked to hear my sophomore or junior year classmates say they didn't know what their major was going to be. Whaaaat??? Didn't they decide when they were three?, I wondered in complete disbelief. It was not until my thirties, when I became a foster parent and started hanging out with three-year-old children, that it really struck me: Holy Cow! I was their age when I decided what I wanted to be when I grew up. That was the first time God spoke to me directly. (Just a hint: It's a good idea to pick up the phone when God calls or He'll resort to other tactics to get your attention.)

Back then, our tiny mountain town and cute little neighborhood was safe for anyone, even dogs, to roam unattended. My brother and I walked to school and Noche walked with us. After she was sure we were safe in our respective classrooms, she would go home—or better yet, to visit our neighbors Lena and Fred, who always stashed treats for her. Noche had no shame; if you gave her a Scooby snack once, she was your BFF. Towards the end of the day she would come back to school to pick us up. We could always count on Noche for punctuality.

The first day of First Grade my teacher, Mr. Simpson, looked out the window and asked if anyone knew the dog outside the door. I looked up, saw Noche, and claimed her immediately. That information led to an invitation, and Noche spent the last part of the day sprawled next to my desk.

We all loved Mr. Simpson—he was kind and sweet. His soft heart was probably why his nerves got the best of him his first day teaching and he had to run out of the room to vomit. Little did he know he had nothing to worry about! Another thing that set him apart was that he ate something called y-o-g-u-r-t... unheard of in 1970 outside of one of those crazy hippie communes. Mr. Simpson was quite worldly and ahead of his time.

We loved Vermont, and my mom, brother and I were devastated when my dad accepted a job as a college professor in the Catskills, near Monticello, NY. But it was there that my mom was able to purchase her dream house in 1971. It was a real fixer-upper and my dad's nightmare house.

107 Main, the early years

He felt those type of things should be left to the experts, and was more likely to pick up the "New York Times Book Review" than a hammer. His lack of skill was painfully exposed when his blind friend, Peter, inspected a closet frame my dad built and told him he was off by a quarter inch. He took that as a true and permanent sign that he should stay in his own box and not one intended for tools.

So both of Joanie's dreams came true. Family: check. Home: check. Mission accomplished. Later known simply as "107 Main," the three-story home encompassed nearly 4,000 square feet, seven bedrooms, and a basement with the same footprint as the house. It was built in the early 1900s when they mistakenly thought that plaster and horse hair could serve as insulation. I can tell you it does not, and I spent each winter of my youth on the brink of frostbite.

My mom would tell me to dress more warmly and I would reply that one more sweater would not only make me look like the Michelin Man, but render me immobile, while negatively impacting my circulation. It's just not normal to have to dress for the outside when you are inside. Call me crazy.

After many pennies were saved, real insulation was finally pumped into the walls, raising the indoor temperature to a steamy 53 degrees in the winter. My frugal mom attempted to convince me that was a healthier temperature. Healthier for a polar bear, I thought, but not for a chick with minimal body fat.

Located in the middle of daunting Columbia Hill, the house was once the property of the Knapp Family, owners of the only Christian hotel in what was then known as the Catskill's Borscht Belt (also, the Jewish Alps). The beautiful Victorian hotel sat on top of the hill and the Knapp family owned all the surrounding homes as well.

But when Atlantic City started to bloom and the train stopped coming to Hurleyville, business also stopped coming, and the hotel went bankrupt in the late 1960s. Our neighbors purchased 107 Main in foreclosure and my parents bought it from them for $11,000. That ruined my mom's perspective on the cost of living forever. When I purchased a "gently used" Toyota Corolla in 1997 for $12,000, I was reminded that my high-end fancy-schmancy car cost more than her house!

The Columbia Hotel operated a ski slope directly behind our house back in the day. After the hotel closed we had endless acres to explore, and often did. I took one of my all-time favorite pictures of Noche on one of those hikes.

Our Precious Noche

But one Christmas Eve in the early 70s, we were saddened to watch a massive fire burn the beautiful old Victorian to the ground. Some called it "Jewish Lightning," but even as a kid I found that hard to believe because it was a Christian hotel. In any event, it was incredibly depressing to see the property in ruins after all the stories we were told about its heyday.

Our house was a labor of love for my mom, and each of the 41 years she lived there she worked to improve it. Because she did not work outside the home, money was tight, to say the least, so she did most of the home improvements herself. She painted the living room and study, and wallpapered all but one of the eleven upstairs rooms (some multiple times over the years), the single exception being a paneled bedroom. As far as my mom was concerned, wall-to-wall, ceiling-to-floor wallpaper never went out of style. That probably explains my severe aversion to wallpaper—I'm a paint kind of girl. Easy on, easily covered up and easily changed.

The grounds too were a labor of love and as an avid gardener my mom planned, developed and planted over the decades. She loved to be surrounded by flowers, blooms and growing plants.

Joanie also loved antiques and furniture refurbishing, so our family home was definitely unique. When the Knapp family owned the house, it was used for overflow guests when the hotel was full. The third floor guest room doors still have the original numbers on them and everyone got a kick out of that. So imagine a full basement (home to the washer and dryer), first and second floors, plus a third floor with guest rooms and what used to be my playroom. That was three flights of stairs my mom went up and down constantly (and why my friends would point out in astonishment, "Your mom's calves are cut!"). She was in amazing shape because of those stairs!

During our first summer at 107 Main my godmother, Zizi, her husband and three children (Thierry, JP and Cat) were transitioning between homes in Illinois and Long Island, so they moved in with us. I remember looking out the third floor window of my playroom, checking out this family that I didn't remember meeting as a baby, as they exited their vehicle. Little did I know we would be as close as blood relatives, creating so many memories over the next decades.

We've rejoiced and celebrated together; mourned and grieved together. Their family threads are part of our family fabric. My mom loved having five kids in the house. It was her dream to have six of her own, and when we bought 107 Main, she also dreamed of the grandchildren that would someday enjoy that Home of Homes. There were no terribly pricey antiques in the house, but it was filled with a wealth of love beyond description.

My mom was all about entertaining. Every holiday was an excuse to party. Come to think of it, a bona fide excuse was never needed. Besides the standard holiday parties, Joanie even threw election night parties—totally bipartisan of course—and everyone was welcome. But the celebration was especially sweet when Barack Obama became the 42nd President of the United States! The thank you card from Michelle and Barack for her $25 donation graced the refrigerator, next to our family pictures, for quite some time.

Never ones to miss a party, Kevin and Kaye Cloonan heard about my mom's famous soirées early on and were added to Joanie's Collection. The Cloonans were known to tip back a few martinis and soon became Joan and Serge's global companions. My mom credits them with getting my father out of the house. Serge was dragged on his first cruise kicking, screaming and kvetching. But when he found out he had to wear a tuxedo he was all-in and became an avid and enthusiastic cruiser. Together they went on cruises all over the world and toured Russia, Oslo, Copenhagen, Germany, the Caribbean and Costa Rica.

Joan, Serge, Kevin and Kaye on one of their many adventures

Kaye and my dad had similar personalities, as did Kevin and my mom. They made for an interesting foursome, perpetually entertaining all the spectators around them. Kaye used to say that Kevin and Joanie sounded like an old married couple because they bickered and debated so much.

Kaye, a professor of humanities at the same college as my dad, was a brilliant, funny and warm friend who encouraged me to publish over 25 years ago. I know she is glad to see from Heaven that her encouragement was fruitful.

Diagnosed with ovarian cancer, Kaye went into remission the year before she passed. During that time, she and Kevin decided they better take advantage of the "Big R" and went to Egypt! They never had to worry about their Bucket List—it seemed to me they were constantly filling it, emptying it, and filling it again.

When Kaye's cancer came back full-force, my mom was by her side—a friend, nurse, companion and rock for Kevin too. My mom's only regret was that she went back home one day, and Kaye left her body during the night. My mom desperately wanted to be with Kaye when she passed to Heaven and hold her hand on the way. We never imagined then that just two years later, my mom would receive the same diagnosis.

My mom collected a vast array of friends over her lifetime and stayed close to many of them. Sue and Ken Kantor were two of our earliest friends after we moved to 107 Main. Ken was another fellow professor and they had two children, Merisa and Todd. Merisa eventually provided Joanie with two fill-in granddaughters, Lexi and Coley.

Lexi and Coley

Although Merisa moved to Florida as an adult, her heart remained in Hurleyville, and she took the girls to spend summers there with her parents. Joanie was, and always will be, a big part of Lexi and Coley's young lives. Among the many lessons, she taught them which wildflowers were tasty to eat—and more importantly, not poisonous.

When my mom put in a four-foot aboveground pool, Lexi and Coley enjoyed it as much as she did. Each of their lives was made rich with so many memories together. Lexi and Coley will carry those memories with them always. More about these amazing little girls, and the threads that contributed to the breathtaking tapestry that was my mom's life, later.

* * *

Winters in the Catskills could be brutal and the mountain roads were treacherous at night. One year my parents invited fellow professor Dr. Richard Dunn to stay over on Wednesday nights since his evening class ended late, and he lived far from the college...over the mountains and through the woods. Dr. Dunn had the honor of staying in Room #18 on the third floor and refused to give Joanie the breakfast orders she requested because he didn't want to be a bother. My mom was a great hostess and Richard always said he could never repay her hospitality. He would come to learn that he was wrong. He and his wife, Kathryn, outdid themselves when it truly counted.

Years later, they purchased a pied-à-terre just two blocks from Sloan-Kettering in NYC. When the Dunns learned my mom was being treated at Sloan, they offered their keys and priority whenever our family needed a place to stay—and were so thankful they had an opportunity to reciprocate the kindness Joanie had shown so many years before. What are the chances? Divine intervention? I know so.

Our family home at 107 Main was an hour-and-a-half at best from Sloan and it was just too much for my mom to spend the day in the city getting chemotherapy treatments or seeing her doctors, and then make the drive home. A convenient hotel room could easily cost $400 a night, and with weekly chemo treatments or lengthy hospital stays, this would have added up quickly. What an amazing godsend the Dunns have been.

****

Growing up with New York winters was no fun for me. I think I suffer from that disease where you need a certain amount of sunlight and warmth to stay sane. In 1997, I decided to make the move to Florida. In retrospect, I find it hilarious that my dad was the biggest protester, never having visited Florida before. He told me in no uncertain terms that Florida was not for me, it was for old people who play shuffleboard all day, and I was certifiable if I chose to move there.

Nonetheless, my father drove to Florida with me and my cat, B-Mo, after my mom threatened him and gave him no choice but to help me move. Two days into the stay, while soaking in the 95-degree hot tub (he thought it felt "cool" to get out into the 93-degree heat) he instructed me to call my mom and tell her to send his clothes—he was staying!

With my dad's new-found love for Florida, and their precious daughter having made the premature move to Retirementville, where old people go to die, they had no choice but to become snow birds. From 1998 on, my dad continued to make his case for living in Florida fulltime and they toyed with the idea of selling 107 Main. But it would never come to be during my mom's lifetime. She absolutely refused to take a penny less than $600,000 for the house she worked so hard to perfect. Never mind the collapsed economy of the entire area, a dead real estate market and comps at $150,000!

Chapter 2

It was the summer of 2009 and my mom knew something "just wasn't right." She visited her gynecologist and got a clean bill of health. Her stomach was upset and stools were flatter than normal. She visited a GI doctor but tests showed nothing and she was declared normal. But she knew something was terribly wrong with her body. She always had boundless energy and now felt tired all the time.

My mom was a textbook case of healthy living. She did everything right. She ate wheat germ, whole grains and took vitamins long before Dr. Oz told us to. With three sets of stairs, a huge house and grounds to keep up, she was always in good physical shape too. In the fall of 2009 she finished a series of doctors' appointments and everyone said she was fine, so my parents came to Florida to spend Christmas with me. At the time, I was running one of the largest public animal shelters in the country and my parents always went in to volunteer when they visited. I still feel bad that I guilted my mom into bathing our shelter dogs even when she said she was too tired. Looking back, I should have insisted she see a doctor in Florida. But she decided to wait until she returned to New York in March and that delayed the diagnosis and subsequent treatment of her cancer, which is never a good thing. Never let the sun set on cancer treatment. Early detection and intervention is key.

Ovarian cancer is difficult to diagnose, which means it is likely found only after it has metastasized and is therefore harder to treat. It's rare to diagnose ovarian cancer with a routine Pap smear and is often mistaken for gastrointestinal disease early on. The take-home message is to listen to your body and have more confidence in your gut feelings than you do in a doctor who tells you everything is fine when you know it's not.

One day in the spring of 2010, I got one of those calls that change everything. I was making dinner and picked up the phone when it rang. My mom told me that a CAT scan had revealed a tumor in her omentum—that's the fatty tissue between our intestinal loops. The tumor was typical of metastatic ovarian cancer, the same disease that took her close friend Kaye Cloonan to Heaven just four years earlier. As a doctor of veterinary medicine, I know that a true diagnosis cannot be made without a biopsy and examination of cells under the microscope. Through my tears I told her I couldn't believe it until the biopsies were done and confirmed, but she gently and lovingly told me she knew it was true.

Our friends and family were in a state of shock. How could Joan— the ultimate health nut, the vitamin pusher, the holistic one, the healthiest of us all—be a cancer patient? It made no sense. If Joan had cancer, many of them said, they'd give up trying to be healthy.

One of my parents' dear friends, Lorena, suffered a stroke in her 30's. If you know anything about stroke victims, it's common to lose certain parts of your personality or ability to censor your opinions. You tell it like it is. When Lorena learned of my mom's cancer diagnosis, she told my father the story of the "disgusting soup." Apparently my mom made some sort of healthy soup and told Lorena it would prevent cancer. When Lorena recounted the story for my dad, she told him, "That soup smelled like garbage! I told Joan I would take my chances and see...look what happened to her, she *got* cancer!"

In June that year, my mom was admitted to Sloan-Kettering; the tumor was removed and her abdomen explored. Her surgeon reported that her entire abdomen, the lining of all the organs and the inside of her abdominal cavity, was covered with tiny tumors she compared to "sprinkled confectioner's sugar." That was bad.

Being a super-organized anti-procrastinator (if you recall), my mom was anxious to have any and all cancer "just cut out." She told her surgeon not to be shy—if she was unsure if something should come out, she should err on the side of taking too much.

Unfortunately, her type of metastasis couldn't simply be cut out. It's like telling someone to remove all your skin. My mom seemed to struggle the most with that concept. I finally suggested that perhaps her surgeon could give her an epidural so she could watch the operation and act as advisor. Can you spell c-o-n-t-r-o-l f-r-e-a-k? My mom's response: "Oh really, they can do that?!" Then I had to break it to her that I was only kidding.

After recovering from a total hysterectomy, my mom started chemotherapy treatments that lasted the next year-and-a-half and included a variety of protocols. Good CAT scan reports were quickly followed by bad CAT scan reports, and we remained on a rollercoaster of alternating highs and lows so typical with serious illnesses. My mom was unfazed by the lows and accepted that her time was most likely limited. She never cried or felt sorry for herself. She never questioned why she was stricken with this deadly disease after having taken such good care of her body.

I think part of her peace came from always feeling like she didn't belong here, in a spiritual sense. She knew for sure she was going to Heaven and accepted the upcoming transition with no sadness, only curiosity.

In August of 2011, a CAT scan revealed that she had more inoperable tumors growing in her abdomen. So that fall my mom decided she wanted to visit Lourdes, France, the world-renowned place of healing where St. Bernadette had visions of the Virgin Mary in 1858.

Having just resigned from my extremely stressful government job, I decided to make the trip with my parents. It was my duty! Someone had to watch out for them...right?

We booked a tour with a company which I will not name because I was very disappointed with their services and don't want to give them free advertising. Each traveler got a backpack with the company logo on it to easily identify the group. But when we arrived at Kennedy airport on our way to France, we saw no other backpacks until we spotted a young lady, around 20 years old, across the crowd. My mom noticed she was alone and instructed me to "go get her!" so we could keep her company.

Her name was Jewel and she was, in fact, traveling alone. The oldest of six children from the Bronx, Jewel suffered from a chronic disease since childhood. She too was going to Lourdes for healing. So the Pizanos (of course) adopted Jewel for the trip. Why did you think I was ordered to go get her?

Jewel and Joan in Lourdes, France, 2011

At that time, my mom was suffering from severe joint pain, a side effect of her most recent chemo drugs. Though we stayed in the famous Grand Hotel Moderne, built by St. Bernadette's brothers very near the holy place of the apparitions, it was painful for my mom to walk, so we requested a wheel chair.

Despite being "sort of" raised Catholic (don't tell my mom I said that!) I had no idea who St. Bernadette was. Perhaps some of you don't either, so let me take a moment to explain the story of Lourdes to my fellow heathens:

Bernadette Soubirous was born in the predominantly Catholic village of Lourdes in southwestern France. In February 1858 while collecting kindling in the woods, she had a vision of a "small lady" in a grotto. Bernadette experienced a total of eighteen visions of the lady, who later called herself the Immaculate Conception. Everyone thought the fourteen-year-old was nuts. She was ridiculed and threatened by the townspeople, and the police wanted to throw her in jail. They never actually arrested her because they couldn't find a law against saying you had a vision.

But many people who believed began following Bernadette to the grotto and witnessing miracles during or after her visions. During one apparition, the lady told her to drink the water near the grotto. In her trance, Bernadette did not realize she was actually eating mud. Even the believers doubted her sanity after that incident.

The next day though, a well of fresh, clean, clear water came up from the ground on that spot, and the spring remains to this day. The lady told Bernadette these would be healing waters, and when she repeated the words to those around her, a desperate mother dipped her incurably ill baby boy into the spring. He was healed immediately and completely. The doctors could not explain it.

The town priest did not initially believe her and slapped her across the face for lying. He told her she better quit being a prankster (I'm paraphrasing here) but Bernadette calmly said (and this is my favorite line), "My job is to give you the message of prayer and repentance. It is not my job to make you believe."

The spring waters continue to miraculously heal the sick. To date, there have been 67 cures considered "worthy of belief," although I am sure thousands of others did not meet the man-made guidelines of a "true" miracle.

More than five million Christians of all denominations make the pilgrimage to Lourdes each year in hopes of a cure for whatever ails them. Each night thousands walk in a candlelight procession, singing hymns of thanks and praise. It is unspeakably breathtaking and beautiful to behold, regardless of how you choose to worship. If you ain't stirred there, I suspect your heart ain't beating and you should see a cardiologist immediately.

With so many people in search of cures, a number of lodgings for the ill exist near the grotto. They are a cross between hotels and hospitals and they attract hundreds of volunteers to help those in wheelchairs or stretchers through the procession, into church services (conducted in a beautiful and endless litany of languages) or into the healing spring waters. We didn't stay there. What did you think... that Joanie was sick or something?

Joanie was quite pleased with herself to be in a wheelchair during that time. In Lourdes, The Sick go to the front of the line automatically. Joanie figured this cancer thing should provide some sort of perks, so whip out that handicap parking sticker—we are getting a good spot today!

Baths for dipping in the healing waters are right next to the grotto and several times a day volunteers help people in and out of the icy water. Be warned—healing in Lourdes is very cold. I did go in, but when invited a second time I said, "I'm healed enough, thank you very much! Where did you say that heated towel was?"

But Joanie went in the bath several times during our stay, and by the time we left, her joints were pain-free and she walked just fine!

There are also fountains where you can drink the sacred waters and believe you me, plenty of tchotchke stores selling containers to collect said water. Do not get me started! I can feel my blood pressure rise as my personal visions of Mother Mary become a blur of statues and images ranging from the size of a pinhead to over twenty feet tall. There are Virgin Mary buttons, flashing lights, candles, key chains, snow globes (seriously)... STOP! Wasn't there something in the bible about not worshipping idols? Did people skip over that part? It's truly sickening but like I said, don't get me started! It would be nice if the Holy Euro was relegated to the outskirts of town to allow visitors to concentrate on miracles at the grotto.

But overall, sans tchotchke, we had a lovely time with our adopted daughter, Jewel from the Bronx. When we returned to the States and went to Joanie's next oncology visit, the CAT scan showed no sign of the tumors detected before the trip! Her doctor could not explain it, but knew we had gone to Lourdes and was more than happy for God to help him out with a miracle. This was no time for egos.

CHAPTER 3

Unfortunately, our joy over the CAT scan and success of the Lourdes trip was short lived. In January 2012 my mom had a permanent intravenous catheter (called a Mediport) put in so she could receive IV fluids at home to prevent dehydration. In February, several tumors began to obstruct her intestines, causing a great deal of pain. She was admitted to Sloan-Kettering again but this time we were told there were no surgical alternatives.

I was living with my boyfriend, Roy, in Miami and taking some time off between jobs. I knew this was bad news and Roy and I decided I should get a one-way ticket to New York to see what was going on and what I could do to help. Since Roy has his own business and for the most part a flexible schedule, we decided it was best for him to stay in Miami for the time being. Roy's mom lived in New Jersey at the time and at almost ninety-years-old, wasn't doing so hot herself. His trips became dual purpose to see both his beloved moms.

This was the first hospital stay when we realized we were not going to get ahead of the cancer. The doctors spoke to us about quality of life, being pain-free and comfortable. Nobody ever mentioned quantity of life and I knew my mom would never ask a question like that. But I had decisions to make and needed an honest answer.

One day, I cornered the oncology team in the hallway and flat-out asked them to level with me. They said that patients in my mom's condition usually lived two-to-three months, but since she was so physically strong they expected her to live a little longer.

I had to ask them the gory details about how things would progress. I needed to know if she could potentially rupture her intestines.

I needed to know what to watch for if I was going to be her main caregiver. They don't tell you everything you need to know or what to expect unless you ask. Being a Type A personality and a Triple A some days, I needed the information so I could emotionally prepare myself, our family and friends; and both emotionally and physically prepare my mom.

The oncology team told me that with this type of disease, the tumors eventually block the intestines until no food can pass or be absorbed and therefore no nutrition is received. Intravenous fluids provide no nutrition, only glucose and/or electrolytes that are essential for brain function. The doctors said her bowels would not rupture, which made me feel slightly better on a scale of one-to-ten. Ultimately, she would become weaker and weaker and die from lack of nutrition. As disturbing as this information was, it helped me schedule my worry appropriately and provide better care for my mom.

At that time my brother, Ra, was working in Antarctica for five months. He'd been there several times over the years and loved it. In this latest job he was responsible for the logistics of loading airplanes leaving "the ice." It was an important job because if you have uneven weight, the plane tips over in the air. Being a veterinarian, and a frequent flier, I can tell you with all certainty that would not be good. Because there are specific times of year that planes can take off and land, Ra was not due back for a few weeks.

When my mom was admitted to the hospital, it was just my dad and me with her. We stayed at 3V, the Dunn's pied-à-terre down the street. Our many friends and family were on pins and needles, so my dad and I found ourselves frequently on the phone, relaying the details of whatever the oncology team had said that day.

For me, it became more and more emotionally difficult to speak, and give updates over the phone. The news was not good and repeating it was to repeat my own pain. Hearing our loved ones cry on the other end was an added measure of piercing heartbreak. So I started a group email list to keep everyone up-to-date, and that is why you're reading this book—the one I accidentally wrote.

The first few email updates were all bad news and grim findings. But later in the day, after I'd hit the send button, something amusing would happen and I would think, "Geez, that was funny—I wish so-and-so could have been here because they missed it and only got gloom and doom today," and I knew that was what would stick in their minds.

So each day I added a funny story about something my mom said or did. Everyone loved being in the loop and my initial list ended up including well over fifty people. Many of those on the original list asked if they could forward the emails to others who were going through something similar. They felt my mom's story would let them know they were not alone and that it was OK to take any opportunity to laugh.

Mostly, I think it is very hard to help a loved one pass to Heaven when they fear death. My mom certainly didn't and I think that made it a little easier for our friends and family. So it became a ripple effect, and The Joan Chronicles were born.

CHAPTER 4

February 23, 2012 7:01 PM
Joanie update

Hi Everyone,

I'm creating an email group since this will be much easier for us to keep you all posted on Joanie's condition.

As you all know, Joanie had a nasogastric tube (NG tube) placed on Tuesday to suction gas and fluid from her stomach that was partly causing the pain and discomfort in her abdomen. She now has three areas of blockages in her intestines, which also cause pain that is most intense when she drinks or eats anything. Unfortunately her intestines become inflamed very easily, which causes the partial obstructions and gas, which also cause pain.

Because her intestines are so diseased, the gas and bloating need to be relieved on a regular basis, and a more permanent solution needed since the NG tube did provide some relief. So today Joanie received a gastric tube (G-tube) surgically. The tube stays in her stomach but is secured with a mushroom shaped piece of plastic that keeps it in place.

The tube exits the stomach and body and is attached to a bag. For one week, this tube must stay open to the bag so the incision site has time to heal. That means that anything she takes in her mouth (liquid or slurry only) will go directly into the bag and she will not receive any nutrition. After that, clamping the tube will be a test when she eats something easily digestible in slurry form. Eating will likely cause further inflammation and obstruction in her intestines.

The only other option for nutrition is TPN or Total Parenteral Nutrition, which is an intravenous formulated nutrition. The intravenous fluids she is already receiving at home only have a little glucose (sugar) and minimal electrolytes but no nutritional content. The problem with TPN is blood infections that can ultimately cause kidney failure are a real risk.

Tomorrow we will be discussing these options with the medical team, as well as the next steps. They may or may not include chemo, depending on what Joanie decides to do. My dad said that someone from hospice came by at the beginning of the week, so not sure when that might happen, but will be finding out before we leave.

Joanie is very much at peace with everything and handling things much better than all of us. We really appreciate all of you—she really feels tremendously loved and so blessed.

At this point, they expect to release us sometime this weekend and I will send a quick update when I know or learn anything tomorrow or as things happen.

We love all of you and are so grateful for your love and friendship!

* * *

When you think of hospice you think death, you think it's the end. To hear it for the first time in the same sentence with your loved one's name feels like you're getting punched in the stomach—really hard. You suspect it may be coming, and you suspect it may be inevitable, but nothing prepares you for that first conversation. But hospice is truly an amazing concept and service. The whole purpose is to make whatever time you have left as comfortable as possible, to give you the best quality of life possible.

I hope more people will think of hospice as a positive thing. We are all going to die: FACT. So since it is inevitable, why not welcome the help to make the transition the best it can possibly be? If you are the person dying at the moment, and are resisting hospice care, I am not asking you to do it for yourself. Do it for your loved ones! They need the help and support, and that relief will free them to love on you more, i.e., you will get better service! You and your loved ones will all benefit.

When we had "the talk" with the social worker in the hospital, my dad was elsewhere and Ra still away so it was just my mom and me. My mom spoke during the conversation like she was talking about fabric softener. I, on the other hand, had tears running down my cheeks, barely able to choke out a question. It was all very hard to talk about. But I do think one thing that helps is to understand how the system works and how it can benefit your loved one and your family and friends. There is a lot of support out there if you need it or chose to use it, so you should never be shy about asking anything.

It was explained to us that we could have as little or as much help from our hospice team as we needed. Roy and I discussed the situation and decided it was best that I stay in Hurleyville and care for my mom. This was not a decision I made out of obligation, but rather, recognizing what a true blessing and amazing opportunity I had to care for my mom, who had always cared for me, our family and friends—unconditionally.

I could help her be more comfortable, prepare whatever meals she could eat and take care of her medical needs. I could help her "finish well." How divinely awesome that I had recently quit my very high pressure job and was free to do that. God had delivered me once again to the right place at the right time. More on that later.

* * *

February 24, 2012 3:31 PM
Joanie update 2

Hi Everyone,
Joanie had the G-tube placed yesterday and the NG tube removed, so is more comfortable today. The G-tube must remain open/patent to the bag it is attached to for one week so the incision can heal. After that she will be on a low fiber diet of super soft or blenderized foods and we will be clamping the G-tube to see how much she can tolerate periodically. The longer the tube can be clamped, the more time her intestines will have to absorb nutrients.

The TPN (described in the first update) is not recommended as the risk of blood infection is very high and it has not been shown to improve either quality or length of life. Joanie decided she will not be getting the TPN. We will not know about any other treatment options/chemo protocols until we speak to the oncologist—probably next week.

We will be released tomorrow and most likely be going to Hurleyville, as long as it's early enough in the day. Ra is now on his way back from Antarctica and will arrive in Newburgh tonight. Each Monday, a nurse will be visiting the house to change the dressing on the G-tube and change tubing on the permanent Mediport she now has. Her care will be managed at home with intravenous fluids daily and the G-tube.

Much, much love and thanks for all your prayers and offers to help— we will be calling on you!

xoxo...

* * *

February 25, 2012 12:34 PM
The Joan

This morning The Joan had a lot of cramping so was nervous to be released. The medical team said that they were fine either way—keeping her another day or releasing her. Because of the drive home and the cramping, she decided to stay another night so tomorrow the plan is to go to Hurleyville. And, drum roll... Ra arrived last night so is safe and sound in the freezing cold of Hurleyville! I'm not certain which is colder—the Antarctic or Hurleyville.

The Joan is able to eat "mechanical soft" and it actually makes her feel full even though most of it goes directly into the bag. Fortunately, she is now even more fashionable because of the gift she received this morning (being a patient at Sloan has not stopped The Joan from being a slave to fashion—her hat/nightie/robe/socks/slippers must match—it's not optional).

Anyway, apparently Evelyn Lauder was a patient here (that would be Estée's daughter-in-law, who ran the company until she passed away last year) and had a G-tube as well. She found it unsightly to look at her gastric contents in the bag and together with her nurse, who just happened to have been a dress-maker, designed a bag to cover it. She has been a big donor here and one of her gifts was a supply of these covers for all the women who have gastric bags, so now Joanie has an official Estée Lauder gastric bag cover!! (Unfortunately no free make-up was included in the bag...I had to ask on behalf of The Joan—she is all about the perks.)

As you all know, everyone loves The Joan. The nurses adore her and call her "Nursie," "Sweetie," "Lovey," etc... The Joan must know the background and life history of everyone she meets—it's mandatory. But last night's exchange turned out to be profitable because one of the nurses, Joyce, is of Japanese descent and they are striking a deal—Joyce is buying some of The Joan's Japanese Girl's Day items! Who needs a garage sale?

Uh oh, The Joan just caught me telling these stories to you and wants to make sure she has some to tell you herself, so I'll leave Bobby-the-Doorman and Randy-the-Nurse Practitioner for her to tell you about. She's instructing me now to report only one funny story per day so we don't run out. Not much time today since the Julliard students are performing at 3 PM then The Descendants playing at 5:30 in the rec room—good thing we didn't leave today because The Joan does not like to miss free entertainment!

Much much love, xoxo...

* * *

February 26, 2012 12:10 PM
The Joan Chronicles #4

The team is here doing the discharge instructions so The Joan will be on the Palisades [parkway] shortly. She's had two good days with minimal/no pain and hasn't needed morphine since Friday morning. She's been eating and feeling full although most of it goes directly out to the bag (now fashionably camouflaged). She's just very tired because you would have a better chance of sleeping in a fraternity house—the hospital is no place to rest.

Here are her current treatments:

- Ativan orally, as needed for nausea or anxiety (I'll be taking that)
- Morphine liquid by mouth as needed (that gets absorbed in the mucous membranes in the mouth and esophagus)
- Intravenous fluids every day for four hours
- Zantac antacid
- Fentanyl patch for pain (gets absorbed through the skin and changed every three days)

Home health care will be coming to Hurleyville every Monday to check on her. Other than that, Joanie is well enough to go up and down the stairs and we have a gastric bag that's smaller that can be attached to her leg with Velcro so she can go out if she wants, and be inconspicuous.

That's your medical update so here's your funny story of the day (even though it happened the other day, remember I had to ration your funny stories).

The Joan requested a visit from one of the hospital priests. Like most doctors here who look like Doogie Houser, he looked about 16 years old— no facial hair whatsoever and I don't think he even has to shave. Anyway, during the "interview" and before any Hail Mary's, the topic of Vermont came up (part of the required historical information) and the priest said he had been to Vermont recently. The Joan asked, "Oh, did you go skiing?" and he sheepishly said, "No, I was visiting a monastery."

Hahahaha! I found this very funny, along the lines of, "Oh, did you go to some nice breweries?" or "Oh, did you go bar hopping after Apri Ski?" Anyway, afterwards when I couldn't stop laughing (not in front of his face, mind you), I said "Balone," (I call her 'Balone' extrapolated from the nickname 'Joanie Bologna'), "Priests don't ski, they vow a life of poverty and can't drop $200 clams for a lift ticket!"... and The Joan replied, as if this was common knowledge and with 100% certainty..."PRIESTS DON'T HAVE TO PAY!" Reeeally? So all you skiers—find yourself a priest to buddy-up with and maybe the Father can get you on the slope for free too!

Color of the day: light blue

Much Love, Xoxoxoxo...

Chapter 5

February 27, 2012 8:44 PM
The Joan Chronicles #5

Since getting The Joan home from the hospital, it's been a little bit of a whirlwind. She's been pretty tired and needed some morphine in the middle of the night for abdominal pain, but didn't need any during the day today. As you know, the G-tube is still open, so a minimal amount of food/nutrition is getting into her system. Much of the food/liquid she eats causes some discomfort though, which is very concerning. Thursday is a turning point because that's when we will be test clamping the G-tube to allow some food/liquid to get into her intestines. If you know of any priests who may be skiing that day, please ask them to Double Pray since they will have some spare time (sorry, you won't appreciate that joke if you didn't receive TJC #4 but I will forward those).

Today, we received visits from two nurses. I didn't realize The Joan would see a nurse from home health as well as Advanced Care. Basically, one nurse (Paul from Advanced Care) will visit once a week and do basic care for the permanent catheter. The second is Debbie, from home health, who checks on her general condition and the G-tube. Apparently each tube from the body requires a different company. Debbie will be visiting 2-3 times a week but was more confident about The Joan's home care givers once I told her I was The Joan's veterinarian. She also got a consult from me regarding her seven-year-old rescue dog that recently had a seizure. I told her I would send my consulting bill to Medicare.

Tomorrow I will start the culinary extravaganza concentrating on high protein/low fiber/high calorie overcooked foods that can be blenderized, mushed or otherwise power The Joan. Wish me luck.

Color of the Day: Light blue and this includes the underwear and if you tell The Joan I told you that I will deny I wrote this and blame Sergie.

We love and adore you all and The Joan loves all your emails and pictures so please keep them coming.

xoxoxo...

* * *

My mom loved to entertain. Now that she was sick and the news was not good, many of our friends and family wanted to visit from near and far. My mom felt tremendous love and support and truly appreciated it, so when loved ones came to visit, she wanted to be "on." This meant she wanted to be awake, not sleepy and not "drugged" so much that she would fall asleep in her tea. But it was a delicate balance of dealing with the pain without the drugs and a continuous struggle. I had to remind her constantly that her comfort was the priority for all her friends and family, period. She fought me constantly about pain control because she did not want to be "dopey" for visitors.

* * *

February 28, 2012 9:07 PM
The Joan Chronicles #6

Hi to all you Joanie fans,

First, the big announcement: Visiting hours are now open 10 AM to 4 PM! Just call ahead of time so there isn't a nurse here dealing with some sort of tubing who will interrupt your quality time. Probably under an hour per visit would be good—she gets very tired but would never admit that to you if you were visiting (another tidbit I will deny telling you).

Also, we have an appointment on Monday, March 5 with The Joan's oncologist— obviously another important turning point so I will take my laptop to the city so I can update you all on Monday night.

I am sorry I can't keep up with telling you who was added to the email list but you'll eventually figure it out and hopefully so will I. I also want to thank everyone for their support of The Joan Chronicles. The Joan has been very adamant that I am annoying you all with way too much information on a daily basis. So I have really enjoyed reading her your responses and more requests for add-ons—some of which include:

"LOVE The Joan Chronicles!"

"This is great information and very witty."

"Where is the update today???"

"What is the Color of the Day?"

"Is no news good news?"

"Can I forward The Joan Chronicles to _____?"

"I'm learning so much about theology."

And something from my cousin Mark about how some priests do have the cash to ski—he's such a good Catholic boy, he knows these things.

This is just the type of encouragement I need to continue TJC. Today was a good day for the following reasons: (1) no morphine needed overnight (2) The Joan got dressed! (Everyone knows only sick people stay in their nighties all day.)

So with that, we will start with the Color of the Day because that is your funny story today—remember Joanie has a limit on the funny stories (one per day) so you'll have to speak to her about Bobby-the-Doorman or beg for the picture of the two of them, which she forbids me to send you. Now get your minds out of the gutter, we were on York Avenue and Sergie was there too—something about her being pale and wearing glasses. And also, I'm not supposed to tell you a lot of personal information like when something happens that rhymes with "bass." Let's just say, I was talking out loud (my first mistake) about how I had to update you about her intestinal motility because that's good news and she hit me! She hit me hard! Make no mistake, The Joan has not lost muscle mass and could likely beat me in an arm wrestle today.

Color of the Day: light green sweater and black pants

Black pants?!?! What was that noise? Did the earth just stop rotating? Are we going to Cultural Affairs at the college tonight? (Side bar for those of you not blessed to have lived in Sullivan County in the 1970s: Cultural Affairs to Joanie is like Lincoln Center is to NYC. Women got d-r-e-s-s-e-d. But you have to think circa 1969 before women started burning their bras and when they wore gloves and hats to church… mind you, no longer a trend but one that The Joan still finds disturbing and refuses to accept.)

Anywho, the point is—black is reserved for formal attire. So how did this happen on a night where there is no Cultural Affairs or Lincoln Center event? The Joan came up with a brilliant solution to comfy clothing. Since her abdomen is bloated and often uncomfortable, not to mention the G-tube sticking out, she decided that she should get maternity pants. So our good friend Susan Kantor, PS (our Personal Shopper), was assigned the task of purchasing The Joan's maternity pants. This expedition quickly turned into an ulcer-producing event. Where to go? There's no Playtogs and no Greene's. (Don't even bring up that department store to The Joan. She is still traumatized that it closed in 1983.)

So off Susan went to the new and improved Middletown Galleria in search of maternity clothes in The Joan's size and signature colors: beige, beige or maybe off-beige for a really crazy day. But **GASP** hot pink, Lady Gaga, low cut, tight fitting non-Joanie attire prevailed. So Susan preceded her display of newly purchased garments with the disclaimer and plea for The Joan's understanding: "Don't forget, Joan," she started, "Most pregnant women are in their 20s!!'" Welcome to 2012, Joanie! You are now fashionable!

And finally reason #3 that it was a good day: The Joan went for a walk around "the neighborhood," but I might have to clarify this one. "The neighborhood" on Columbia Hill in the winter means she walked up and down the driveway. Sad but true, but she did do several laps with Ra and Sergie and liked being out in the sun.

So thank you for listening and thank you for caring. I really appreciate your encouragement and, truthfully, really look forward to writing The Joan Chronicles because it's been a good distraction for me and hopefully for you too. And for those of you encouraging me to publish, please get on that right away so I can work from home and get really rich like Stephen King.

Much love from the Pizanos...

* * *

February 29, 2012 6:28 PM
TJC #7

Hello Loved Ones!
   Another semi-pain-free day but don't forget, the G-tube is still wide open. To power The Joan takes two times Shrek's menu and that's per hour—it is a full time job. Tomorrow is National Clamp and Double Pray Day so don't forget, banks and some government offices may be closed. That will be a huge turning point one way or the other.
   We did have a discouraging morning when The Joan got on the scale. Admittedly, we haven't done this daily but I could have told you there would be weight loss—I am a veterinarian, you know. She was 107 pounds when she went into the hospital last week and today 100.2 pounds. If you saw her I don't think that you would think she was very ill. She has good color in her face and... well... let me paint the complete visual for you:
   As you know, The Joan has the ever so fashionable and functional Evelyn Lauder G-tube bag cover. What I didn't tell you is that while she is walking around the house, she puts the loop on the top of the bag over her wrist. It looks like she is carrying a little pocketbook if it wasn't for the tube with the gastric juices leading up to the "purse," and there's no lipstick or credit card in there, I can tell you that much. So last night I wanted to make a nice family dinner in the dining room and serve versions of what she was eating to everyone.
   Knowing this, The Joan started to tidy up (while on IV fluids, mind you). The one-liter IV bag with a tube connected to her catheter is hanging from an IV pole on wheels so she is mobile as can be if necessary. (Side note: Giving The Joan IV fluids is not a problem for me since it's exactly the same as a dog or cat. The only difference is that we veterinarians find it safer to put those little ill pets in cages while attached to those IV fluids.)
   Back to the story: So The Joan was tidying up and saying things about certain people in the family (I don't want to name names or place blame but I will say "gender: male") and fluttering around like she was attached to nothing and like it was perfectly normal to have tubes coming out of her and she... she... she... opened the basement door!!! In a brief moment of panic, I thought "Mother of Josephine, she is going to go down those basement steps with that IV pole!" I was about to do a volleyball dive in

front of her to block her and inhaled deeply to brace myself for potential impact when... she did a 180 and continued on about "members" of the family leaving dirty laundry in front of the door. Phew, close call.

So after dinner I ordered a crate online and from now on, The Joan will get those IV fluids in a secured cage. It's the only safe thing to do and I know you will all agree with me! Again, please call before you visit.

In closing, I wanted to share with you that my cousin, Mark, the good Catholic boy that he is (hard to believe but he was an altar boy!) has confirmed that priests do have to pay for lift tickets and thank you to cousin Thierry for enlightening us about our Polish brothers and fathers: http://www.metro.co.uk/news/855652-priests-take-to-polands-ski-slopes-to-compete-in-annual-clergy-race.

Color of the Day: pink and... black! (but now you were prepared appropriately)

Much, much love and please call if you feel like it. Everyone is afraid to call but it's OK—just don't stay on too, too long because it takes a lot out of her. She needs to conserve her energy for important tasks and if The Joan is scrubbing the bathroom floors, we'll just have her call you back when she's done.

xo...

* * *

March 1, 2012 5:30 PM
TJC #8

Hurdle No. 1) We clamped and no cramps!
This morning The Joan had a high protein banana/Greek yogurt shake for b'fast and then we clamped the G-tube for a half hour. The no-cramp response was very good since any-and-everything she ate or drank prior to last week was giving her severe cramps. We clamped again for high protein carrot soup this afternoon. (Who knew ricotta cheese had more protein than tofu? Not me—I'm still dizzy from reading labels at Shoprite) and voila! No cramps. Triple phew.

Hurdle No. 2) The next 48 hours, as the items in paragraph one and tomorrow's menu move through the GI tract.

The Joan is very tired and even talking on the phone for long periods of time wears her out. I feel that I am helping in my own small way by giving you all the pertinent information so if you do speak to her, you can have quality talk time. The Joan begged to differ until today when she lifted censorship and in addition, gave me permission to send the Bobby-the-Doorman picture! I'll do that tomorrow so you have something to look forward to.

And speaking of censorship, The Joan was getting a little testy because I was reading your email responses and she wasn't getting the jokes because she has not been getting The Joan Chronicles herself. I figured, you know, she's living it, so why does she have to see it in print? Today, however, I was forced to print them all for her to read so if you do not receive TJC tomorrow, rest assured I was kicked out of the house or the laptop was thrown out the window. If you don't hear from me, please call 911 on my behalf.

Now for some other business we need to discuss: The Color of the Day. Today, The Joan is wearing a cream sweater and another pair of black maternity pants (which may explain why she does the labor breathing exercise when she does get a cramp), a black and grey cap and.... a coral silk scarf with a pearl clasp (for color, she said). She is ready for the Sloan-Kettering Fashion Week Runway.

So my dear friends and family, this is why I am ending this wildly popular segment today. I know, I know... you wait all day for it and Nicole even dresses her four month old in honor of Joanie's palette of colors, but The Joan is now aware that the Color of the Day is popular and that everyone is "watching." I don't want her to have any pressure on her and I want to encourage her to mismatch in the name of comfort. She was waaaay too dressed up today (like Cultural-Affairs-dressed-up).

To replace the Color of the Day, I am introducing a new segment tonight that I know you will appreciate immensely. Not only that, The Joan's palette is quite finite, if you know what I mean, but I have enough material for this next segment, that, if written end to end, will stretch from the earth to the moon and back:

JOANIE'S PEARL

As you know, The Joan is chock full of nuggets—Pearls of Wisdom that none of us could survive without. Here's the first one:

Sara Pizano, MA, DVM

"When making batches of cookies at Christmas, make the cookies small. That way, you can taste ALL the different types of cookies and not get stuffed after eating only one."

Good night our sweet friends and family—it's nearing 5 PM. I have to go now—it's supper time, aka "the early bird special." When in Rome...

xo...

CHAPTER 6

My mom overflowed with advice about everything from removing stains to treating poison ivy. She had shortcuts for everything and she would throw out pearls of wisdom endlessly. I am saying in all sincerity that every Christmas since my birth, my mom would tell me how she makes a variety of small Christmas cookies each holiday. We're talking decades of repetitive-couldn't-forget-if-I-tried cookie size advice.

One Christmas, I must have been in my early forties at the time, I was in Hurleyville and pitching in with the cookie making. Now I like a meaty, multiple-bite kind of cookie and my cookie size reflects that. Plus, weight gain is mandatory at the holidays, right? Just my dad and I were in the kitchen and I predicted, "When mom walks in the kitchen, she will look at the cookie sheet and tell me that she always makes the cookies small, so everyone can sample all of them." On cue, my mom walked in the room, looked at the cookie sheet and said, "You know... I always make the cookies small so everyone can sample all of them." With that, Serge and I erupted into fits of laughter, but the kicker was what she asked me next: "Oh, did I tell you that before?" I answered, "Uh-yaaah."

So Joanie's Pearls began to take on a life of their own with friends and family reminding me of all those pearls that were shared with them over the years, sending us their own pearls or requesting clarification of a pearl. I had always thought that I would one day compile all Joanie's Pearls in a book for her friends, but never would I have imagined the road I would take to get there, no less posthumously for her.

* * *

Sara Pizano, MA, DVM

March 2, 2012 8:28 PM
TJC #9

Hello Dear Friends and Family,

Today The Joan had a pretty good day but last evening was not so great. The Joan had to take oral Ativan and morphine for the second night in a row because of the spasms (a note to all you insomniacs, The Joan reports that she slept very well).

Today's activities included clamping three times (½ hour, ½ hour and 1 hour) and so far, so good. The Joan especially enjoyed my newly-developed recipe, The Mashed Potato Shake. Yes, you heard it here first so if you see it on Rachael Ray's show, she stole it from me. The Joan was craving carbs so for all my fellow and/or recovering carboholics, here's the recipe:

Very well cooked and mashed potatoes, butter, sour cream, tofu, protein powder and Lactaid. Put all in a blender and blend well, then strain through a super fine strainer. The Joan reports it was delicious!

And... drumroll... As promised, The Joan lifted censorship and is allowing this one picture to be sent to you (you know, like the Kardashians and "People" magazine, we have to have some control over information and limit what goes out). I am attaching the picture of Joanie right after she was released from the hospital on Sunday with her beloved "Bobby-the-Doorman." We are so incredibly blessed to have such amazing friends in our lives and the Dunns have been so gracious to let us stay in their city apartment while The Joan was getting treated or in the hospital. It's three blocks down the same avenue from the hospital! Thank God!

Anyway, now you know the connection with Bobby-the-Doorman. He and Joanie have this mutual crush going on and when The Joan told him the next step was Mary Jane/pot/weed/grass in the brownies, he said, "Get my room ready, I'm coming to visit!" I apologize for my iPhone label on the bottom but I am a veterinarian, not a techie and I couldn't figure out how to delete it without deleting the picture. Remember, everyone has <u>specific</u> gifts, and manipulating photographs on the computer is not one of mine. (Does anyone else miss the anticipation of getting your pictures developed at the drugstore?)

And, before I leave you with a Pearl, I have to make a correction from TJC #8. It turns out The Joan was not dressed up because she felt pressure from the Color of the Day announcement, she was

Cultural-Affairs-dressed-up because we had planned on going to the Home Depot (which turns out to be actually funnier and now I don't feel so bad).

JOANIE'S PEARL
"Eighty percent of the heat from your body goes out the top of your head in cold weather so a hat is <u>absolutely essential!</u>"

Much Love...

Joanie and Bobby-the-Doorman wearing hats

CHAPTER 7

In 1989 my dad was asked to be an exchange professor in Kosugi, Japan, for a year. It was the opportunity of a lifetime and Joanie's only question was: Where do I sign up for this exciting global adventure? That year turned into *four* of the most amazing years of my parents' lives.

They threw themselves wholeheartedly into Japanese culture and were treated like rock stars! Trees were planted in their honor at the local school and rice farmers hosted them on weekends. While Serge taught at the college, Joanie taught English to local Japanese ladies and studied Shiatsu. More lifelong friends were found and added to The Collection and one of them was Brenda Haye. She would go on to marry and have two children who would provide two more fill-in grandchildren for Joanie and Serge. It was a mutual lovefest. My mom made many wonderful friends in Japan that she remained in touch with some 20 years later.

Joan embracing the Japanese culture

Come to think of it, most of my mom's friends were in her life for many decades, like my godmother Zizi. Zizi's daughter, Cat, also supplied a fill-in grandchild for Joanie when little Isabel came along. Isabel was born an old soul and we knew early on that she was very special. At the funeral of her recently deceased Goldfish, her mom told her how sorry she was for her loss. Five-year-old Isabel took her mom's hand and comforted her saying, "It's OK mom, we'll see him on the other side." My mom adored Cat and Isabel too, another lovefest.

Children always held a special place in my mom's heart. In the mid-1980s, after my brother and I left for college, she opened a Montessori-type nursery school in our house. She loved being around little ones and after she passed on to Heaven, several of the parents of those kids stopped by to give us their condolences and told us that even though their children were now adults, they still talked about the amazing experiences at "Joanie's house" all those years later.

* * *

March 3, 2012 4:31 PM
TJC #10

Hellooooo Loved Ones!
    The Joan had a good night and so far, a good day with no cramps... I mean "spasms" (she's now my acting thesaurus and wants me to use the word spasm instead of cramps). Although I am not entirely sure what the difference is, I do not argue with The Joan, I just do what my beloved has taught me, and say, "Yes Dear," if I am asked to accommodate a request.
    So tomorrow we leave for NY and Bobby-the-Doorman. We'll let you know how the appointment with the oncologist, goes... but The Joan is not too keen on continuing chemo. The last round was very hard on her and as you know, it has made her very ill since November. She feels continuing to be sick like that would be too much to handle now. We're going with an open, yet cautious mind.
    Today, Brenda (who some of you know from my parent's days in Japan) and her girls visited, and my cousin Cat is visiting with her daughter Isabel. Isabel is in the 6th grade and although very precocious, I thought I should speak to her on the phone about the IV and the G-tube ahead of time so she wouldn't be freaked out if she saw my mashed potato shake in a tube attached to a bag sticking out of Joanie's abdomen. Cat then told me the following story:
    Isabel pulled her mother aside the other day and said there were two things she needed to discuss with her. One, she wanted to make sure her mother completely understood everything about a G-tube, and proceeded to draw her a diagram and speak in detail about how it worked. She did, however, report that she would not play the online video for her mother since it was "too graphic."
    The second thing was to make sure her mother understood "the birds and the bees," since they were learning about it in school and she thought she could act as a reference for her mother! Haha!
    So my question is this: Helloooooo!? Are there any actual children left on the planet? My friend's three-year-old navigates an iPad better than I do. What happened to Silly Putty?

JOANIE'S PEARL
    "Entertain often and when you do, pre-organize as much as possible so you can have maximum quality time with your

guests. This includes actually labeling the serving dishes on the set table several days before the event to ensure there's a place for each menu item."

With Much Love...

* * *

March 4, 2012 11:31 AM
TJC #11

Aloha from sunny (yet frigid) Hurleyville!
(I'm trying to pull up memories from past Hawaiian vacations to help keep me warm but so far, not working.)
OK—more censorship requirements from The Joan since she read TJC. This morning, The Joan has imposed further regulations on TJC and information-sharing to include:

1) *Cut down on the medical information.*
2) *Nobody cares how long or how many times she's clamped.*
3) *Say only "she had a good day," or "she had a bad day," and leave it at that.*

I pleaded my case with resignation: "But your fan base is <u>demanding</u> this information of me!!" (Which is, BTW, a true statement. On that note, I have found that sometimes clarification is requested, so for the rest of you wanting to know but were afraid to ask... putting The Joan in a dog crate for IV fluids was a joke.)
Anyway, I am left with no alternative but to say "yes dear," and then delete those forbidden parts when I print them for her. Under oath, I can truthfully say the extreme cold (below 75 degrees) is causing brain freeze—think Olive Oil and Jack Nicholson in The Shining.
I really do want to tell you what happened this morning that was of great significance and fabulous news. But due to censorship requirements and the un-lady-like nature of the subject, I can't come right out and say it. I'll just have to give you some hints and hope you are good at riddles. Here goes:

1) It's what we were waiting and hoping for about 48 hours!
2) It was "hurdle number 2" in a previous TJC and sometimes referred to by this number.
3) Everything that goes up must come down, everything that goes in must go out.

I hope you got it—the pressure of having this vital information and not sharing it with you is unbearable. It's very stressful working full time for The Joan—lots of rules you know (can you imagine?). But yesterday—whoa baby, yesterday takes the proverbial cake—let's say that I was rendered speechless, which by now I know you simply cannot fathom. First, I have to give you a little background so you can appreciate the impact of what transpired.

I love to cook. I love to bake. I watch the Food Channel incessantly and it's the home page on my computer. I read cookbooks instead of novels. For Christmas Roy gave me a gift certificate for Boot Camp, not at a gym but at a fancy culinary school. When I cook, I try to make fabulous-tasting food that is super healthy and presented in an aesthetically pleasing manner. If it freezes well—that's perfection.

Now, with The Joan's new limited menu, this has been extra challenging so I am constantly trying to meet all my natural criteria. So, each hour The Joan enjoys a little masterpiece and gets as much pleasure (and protein) out of what she puts in her mouth as possible. I'm trying to make the best out of a bad situation.

Don't get me started on the apricots—I'll tell you about that another time. Suffice to say that The Joan had a craving for apricots and requested apricot baby food. For all you parents of babies, hear this: I suspect Mr. Gerber is in mafia-like with the American Diabetes _and_ Dental Associations. If Oprah asked me what I knew for sure, that's what I would say.

Did you know that in that little tiny bite of a jar of apricot baby food there are 19 grams of sugar!? Somebody should go to jail for that one—just like the tobacco people. I flatly refuse to serve it to The Joan, and while continuing the search for fresh apricots, our good friend Saniye donated a can of apricots with half the sugar. OK—until I get my greasy little paws on the fresh apricots, I'll work with it.

The Joan was getting a little tired of drinking her food when clamped (oops—was that TMI on the medical?) so I put 2 pieces of apricots (not smushed, so she doesn't only get smushed food—remember, it's all about the presentation) on top of a dollop of Greek yogurt. To be extra fancy, I then gently spooned some juice from the can, like a pastry chef at the Russian Tea Room (such a shame, now closed). I presented it to The Joan. She took one look at it and demanded to know in all seriousness—and this warrants its own paragraph for full impact:

"IS THIS A JOKE?!"

I know, I know. You think I am exaggerating or maybe she was kidding but I have a witness! My cousin and I stood in stunned silence with our mouths gaping. Then we started laughing. I returned to the kitchen with my tail between my legs and instead served the rice cake with butter and tea that was ordered to replace my "fancy" snack. It's OK, I once saw Julia Child burn a rib roast. I also read that Babe Ruth struck out like a million times—it happens to the best of us. (Does anyone have the 1-800 number for the Caregivers Union? I need to start paying dues immediately if not sooner.)

JOANIE'S PEARL

"If you are in the passenger seat of a car and need air, crack the driver's window so you get the cross ventilation. If you crack your window, the air will go over your head and you will miss the benefit of the breeze."

We are off to the city that never sleeps and you are all with us.

God bless you, xo...

* * *

March 5, 2012 6:38 PM
TJC #12

To Our Dear Loved Ones,

We are back from NY, and heard from the oncologist what we expected. He said that at this point, The Joan would not be eligible for any clinical trials or experimental chemotherapy because of the intestinal obstructions and the severity of her disease. He laid out two options. The *first was to increase the home care and focus on comfort/palliative care with no further chemotherapy.*

The second was to do another course of one of the chemotherapy drugs used a year-and-a-half ago. That drug would be given again once every three weeks and there would be a 20-30% chance that it could shrink the tumors in the intestines at least for a time. The Joan was happy to be reminded that that drug does not cause your hair to fall out and it didn't make her sick to her stomach, just very fatigued.

Now, before the Pearl, I will quote The Joan's response: ".... OK, that will buy me another few weeks so I can finish my to-do list... there are still some things I need to get organized, you know!" Cancer schmancer, The Joan will stay on schedule.

(Ten minute crying break.)

OK—I'm back—the tears were lined up in my tear ducts from here to Minnesota... unbelievably, it's still so surreal.

JOANIE'S PEARL

"It's OK to collect coins or dolls but your most important collection should be the special people you bring into your life. And once you find those special people, be kind, a good friend, and generous of heart. Be loyal and loving and never hold a grudge. Once you find them, never let them go."

Much Love to The Joan's "Collection"

PS: Please pass the Kleenex, I made myself cry again.

* * *

March 6, 2012 8:17 PM
TJC #13

Hello everyone,

Today has been a pretty good day. The Joan seems to have trouble/ pain late in the afternoon, and lying down for bed is also a problem, which is why she's needed morphine four out of seven nights. Also, her cravings can sometimes create an issue, but she is clamping more often now so getting a little more nutrition. She has, however, lost a total of 20 pounds and is down to 98 pounds.

She is allowed soft cheese that's melted and yesterday had a craving for mac and cheese. Strangely enough, I have never made macaroni and cheese from scratch, so found a trusty recipe from The Barefoot Contessa that I assumed would have plenty of fat.

After the Lactaid and several protein powder scoops—voila! I sat and watched her, waiting for the review... she loved it! (the good news)

It didn't love her (the bad news). Ra said that he could make his version but I told him orange powder from a box would not be served to The Joan under any circumstances!

Tonight, The Joan had a craving for lobster and strangely enough, again, I have never cooked a lobster—whole or part (I could never bring myself to boil a live animal so resorted to the Shoprite frozen food section). But... voila! She loved it! And so far.... it loved her. Another phew. So each day is an experiment and a trial, just trying to see what works best and what doesn't work.

Today was also a great day because my honey-cake, Roy, arrived from Miami and The Joan <u>loves</u> Roy. He brings a Zen to the house, like feng-shui in the form of a person, and I'm fairly certain he'll have us all doing yoga by bedtime. The Joan loves Roy, not just because he's so good to me and is a "good man," as she says, but that man can fix absolutely anything (so he gets the maximum bonus points allowed to boot). Blow dryer broken? No problem, Roy will take it apart and fix it. Something needs to be rewired? Not a problem, Roy can do that. Sergie has seventeen viruses on his computer, Roy can remote in from across the country and save the day. Water gushes through the dining room ceiling and it rains on the dining room table on Christmas day, no problem, Roy will fix it (if you haven't guessed by now, these are not jokes but actual stories!).

Anyway, nothing measures up to the latest. Joanie sent in an application to have him sainted by the Pope, (even though he's Jewish... but remember who else was!) because of this one: For exactly 41 years of winter mornings, The Joan has taken her little tuchus out of her cozy bed (under seven wool throws, an electric blanket set on high and a down comforter) to go down the hall, down the stairs, down another hall and into the dining room to turn the heat to a habitable level and prevent the family's eyeballs from freezing. She followed the reverse path to get back in that cozy bed to doze off until her appointed wake-up time (at this point, I do have to remind you—so you appreciate this whole story—that the phones were "recently" switched to push button from rotary). Anyway, my genius honey inquired, "Joanie, why don't I install a digital thermometer on a timer so the heat can go up and down on its own depending on how you set it?" Voila! Done! And The Joan said it changed her life! (OK, granted, we had to wait for Roy to visit again to actually have it reset and move accurately, but at least it's installed!)

JOANIE'S PEARL
"When you have a garage sale, make sure you place the free pile at the back of the yard so customers have to walk by all the pricey $10 items and don't just take free stuff."

With all our love, xo...

* * *

March 7, 2012 6:14 PM
TJC #14

Dear Loved Ones,
Today has been a trying day but I will still tell you something funny that did happen at the end.
Let's get this over with first: The Joan had a very bad night last night and was in a lot of pain. Her abdomen became very bloated and it seems like any food causes problems. She is down another pound.
This morning the priest from her church called to ask if he could come over with communion and the anointing. The weird thing is that we didn't call him but The Joan was thinking about him, so I think God just set it up for her to make it easier. I also didn't know what the "anointing" meant when he called. In the Catholic faith it used to be the special prayer for the sick but apparently the rule book changed and it means "last rites" too. Wasn't expecting that one today. After the priest left, The Joan announced "OK, I'm ready now, it's just that nobody else is." From her lips to God's ears, ain't that the truth!
Mid-afternoon today she became very painful and nauseous so took both Ativan and morphine and is now sleeping. This is the first day she's needed it

so early and has slept during the day in quite a while. She feels that the cancer is progressing and thus far, she has been right and predicted each CAT scan and test result accurately. So overall, a very tough day.

I was also censored and am not allowed to send you a picture I took of her this morning—something about the lack of lipstick. I begged her so that you would know I'm not making this up, but this is what happened:

Since the Color of the Day segment came to a close, there are still many of you wanting to know what it is. Well, I'll secretly tell you that the COTD today is pale blue (definitely sweater and cap but I cannot confirm or deny underwear color as I did not see it myself and flatly refuse to check for you—definitely not ladylike).

Anywho, this morning, Nurse Debbie from Sullivan County Public Health came to check on The Joan, (Oh! Did I also tell you that Nurse Debbie wants to learn Japanese, so in between blood pressure and bandage change The Joan made another sale of Japanese paraphernalia?!... Now I ask you: What are the chances that a Sullivan County Public Health nurse would want to learn Japanese?!?) and... and... she took out a thermometer with... you guessed it! A pale blue tip! Really, what are the chances that her thermometer matched The Joan's sweater and cap?? All kinds of crazy spiritual things happening here at 107 Main.

JOANIE'S PEARL
"If you wear the same color—for example, a beige hat, beige sweater, beige pants and beige shoes—it will make you look taller."

With much love, xo...

* * *

My mom was five feet tall in stocking feet. I often wondered how much taller she thought she looked when she wore all beige. Did wearing all beige make her feel like she was 5' 7"?, I would ask. I never did get that mystery solved.

* * *

Thursday, March 8, 2012 7:41 PM
TJC #15

Hi Everyone,

  Today was a pretty good semi pain-free day! The Joan took a little snooze/rest this afternoon (she's the type to claim she "wasn't sleeping") and only gave into one craving today—an orange creamsicle that she has been "joansing" for (a Donna Butler joke... I can't take the credit for that one). Now, who ate the first eight of twelve creamsicles remains a mystery, but Roy will be setting up a hidden camera this evening in an effort to catch and subsequently counsel the snacking bandit. Have I not done enough to communicate what is and isn't The Joan's?!?! (See picture of "The Joanie Only fridge") I am asking you: What more can a PC (Personal Chef) do?

Photographic evidence of the "Joanie Only" fridge

I truly believe that after maintaining The Joan in the manner to which she has grown accustomed, I am now fully capable of managing the kitchen at Le Cordon Blue with one hand tied behind my back. Resume builder: Managing The Joan's menu—It may be a tough sell to a potential employer so I may have to include you all as my trusty references (just please don't mention the apricot debacle).

The Joan also completed an important task on her to-do list: collecting and packing Japanese items for an exhibition at the Sullivan County Historical Museum in beautiful downtown Hurleyville. Watch for it at Sotheby's online and the NY Times Art and Leisure section, and get your tickets early.

Today, the Dunns had an audience with The Joan and a lovely visit. The mister was wearing green pants and a coordinating green shirt, which will mean something to you after you finish reading the next segment. (PS: he really did look taller!)

Now extra special today only, and in place of Joanie's Pearls, a bonus: Joanie's Extra Pearls! Susan's granddaughter (Merisa's daughter) seven-year-old Coley, needed clarification about the recently published Fashion Pearl. I will not attempt to paraphrase as the whole thing is hysterical on its own. This will be sort of a Dear Abby thing—The Joan gets a question and then responds. Here is the actual question and answer:

From Merisa:

"Coley enjoyed Joanie's Pearl today about dressing in one color. She asked me if it only works in beige, or if it would work with green or blue. I said if you dressed in green head to toe, you may look like you belong in a crayon box. She told me to please check with Joanie on that because she really needs to look taller, but doesn't like beige."

The Joan's answer (and fashion consultation analysis):

The Joan doesn't want Coley to have to worry about being taller right now because she is still growing. However, she wants her to know that whatever colors (she emphasized the plural) she is happy to wear that day will work! Another piece of advice for Coley is that Joanie says when it's gloomy outside, wear bright colors and reserve the dark colors for sunny days.

Much love...

PS: The Joan is actually wearing beige today! Hahaha.

PSS: OK, now isn't it funny that Dr. Dunn wore green pants and a green shirt? What are the chances? And I am fairly certain that he did not discuss his wardrobe choices with Coley last evening, but I can report that he looked very classy and not at all like a crayon (must have been the hues).

AND THIS JUST IN FROM COLEY TO ME:
"Could you call Keith Peters? He is our principal, and tell him that Joanie said whenever it is gloomy we should wear bright colors, not our uniforms.
Thank you, Coley Lavere"

We laughed until we cried after reading that one!

* * *

Friday, March 9, 2012 9:05 PM
TJC #16

Dear Loved Ones,
Bad day at the office. The Joan's pattern this week has been good day/bad day/good day/bad day, but today was definitely the worst. She woke up very weak and then started to feel nauseous so has not eaten anything to speak of today except ½ cup of a protein shake in the morning and a few Ritz crackers with a cup of tea. Not getting enough calories creates the cycle of weakness.
We've had to give her morphine twice so far since 4 PM and she's feeling very dehydrated, but unable to drink much without it causing pain. We're all hanging out in the bedroom with her now, but wanted to get this out to you, and know you'll understand if I ever miss a day of the TJCs. Hopefully, she'll fall asleep soon.
Kevin says that it's always a good sign if The Joan is organizing or directing and that, I assure you, she is continuing to do between spasms. We're supposed to put an antique desk and chairs on Craig's List at this price, the dresser at that price and the proceeds are to go to this one or that one. I had to leave the room to get pen and paper—my head was spinning.
We are still planning to go to the city on Monday for a chemo treatment and see what happens. In the meantime, pray that the cycle continues and tomorrow will be a good day.

JOANIE'S PEARL
"THERE IS NO TECHNOLOGY THAT CAN EVER REPLACE SNAIL MAIL!"

MUCH, MUCH LOVE...

CHAPTER 8

If you have ever visited central Pennsylvania, you have no doubt seen the row houses or duplexes. Many are stuck directly together, some have a few feet between each two-family house. In 1947 my Nana and Pappy moved to Laurel Street in Minersville when George, Jane and Joan were teenagers. Ducky and Florence Laudeman were on the other side of the row house with their three children: Bill, Janice, and Jim (Gary Lee came later). The Laudemans and the Hahns grew up together and were very close. So close in fact, that the attic had no separation so the kids could cross over to each other's homes!

My Nana and Florence had been friends since high school and their friendship would remain strong for over 70 years. I guess my mom and Bill had a thing for a while in their youth, and when Jimmy was little he begged to go on a date with them. Bill said an unequivocal and final "NO," but when Jimmy asked my mom, she said "Of course!" and the date became a threesome, much to Bill's dismay.

Janice and Joanie were close friends their whole lives too, even though they later lived in different states—Joan in NY and Janice in Delaware. But each year, starting in 1998, they would meet as snowbirds in Florida to party hearty. That crew had a social life to rival all others!

My mom remained connected to many close friends over the years. She even saved love letters from Skip (her 1957 high school boyfriend), whom she kept in touch with until she passed. In one, he told Joanie about Janice's beau that she was going to marry. Skip thought he was a good guy and—thank goodness—Janice and Tip Sukeena have been married ever since.

* * *

Sara Pizano, MA, DVM

Saturday, March 10, 2012 8:07 PM
TJC #17

Hello to The Joan's Collection,
    True to form, The Joan kept her schedule of good day/bad day, and had a good day today but with mindful strategic planning. She awoke unusually early (6:30 AM), no doubt in anticipation of her sister (Jane), niece (Michelle) and her family's scheduled visit. (I know! A miracle! Pigs just flew!) She showered and we started her IV fluids early and she snoozed/rested until they arrived at 11 AM so she would be ready for the day's festivities.
    The Joan had a blast, as expected, and spent most of her time having everyone pick something from her jewelry collection, Japanese collection, etc. (and explaining why they should like it) so she knew they would get something special from her. I had to draw the line when I saw my cousin Jonah eye the brand new TV in the living room. Anyway, it proved to be the best medicine for The Joan.
    After our family (and Roy, boohoo) left, The Joan took another snooze/rest, had another high protein power snack and is off to bed now with a little morphine for good measure. We will be repeating the schedule tomorrow with the Sukeenas of Delaware and the Laudemans of Pennsylvania—can't wait.
    Side bar: Aren't you proud of The Joan for allowing the purchase of a new TV? It all started when I was watching the tube (and I mean "tube") captivated by some fascinating program like "Antiques Roadshow" and the sound went out. The Joan nonchalantly instructed me to hit the top left part of the TV. For all you young'uns out there, in the old days TVs used to be the shape of a box!
    Anywho, I obediently hit the top _left_ side and voila! the sound came on... but then the picture went fuzzy. No fear, The Joan instructed me to hit the top _right_ part of the TV. Reluctantly, I did and then sent Serge to Middletown with his trusty electronics advisor, Roy, to purchase a beautiful thirty-nine-inch flat screen TV! I told you, miracles happening every day here at 107 Main.
    I just remembered that "107 Main" is funny to me but not to you—I have to explain so when I refer to this house in future chronicles, it will make you chuckle too. Recently, along with the switch to the push button phone from rotary (still has a cord but progress is slow here in the mountains) someone,

somewhere decided that identifying this house with a post office box in town was no longer appropriate and they were only doing that now for families entering the witness protection program.

The Fed Ex man with his iPad simply refused to accept directions that started with "make a left at the big field after the second old oak tree" (not to be confused with "the young oak tree"). So we were given a <u>real</u> street address!!! 107 Main Street, baby!!! Unfortunately, Fed Ex still can't find us because they always think that Main Street is in town and once they leave town they have gone way too far. Anyway, the Pizanos think it's super-cool to have a street address so I have to refer to it as often as possible.

JOANIE'S PEARL

"If you have a wrap-around drive, all cars should be facing towards the road so you pull out head first. This is particularly important during the winter so when you get snowed in you can floor it and get out."

Much Love...

* * *

Sunday, March 11, 2012 8:22 PM
TJC #18

To all The Joan's People,
The Joan woke up very tired this morning and is down to 94.6 pounds. I believe part of the weight loss this week is that she is dehydrated, even though she is getting one liter of intravenous fluids a day. Tomorrow I will be asking her oncologist (who we see at noon) if we can increase her fluids a little since she can't drink enough to make up for it—she's still super thirsty and we want her to be as comfortable as possible.

After seeing the doctor, she will receive another dose of chemo. Once we resolve her dehydration, her weight should be a little bit higher. She was able to eat some egg soup (yum!) for breakfast and an orange creamsicle, which is now a daily staple, and some other high protein mush.

So today, we did similar strategic planning in preparation for the Laudemans of Pennsylvania and Sukeenas of Delaware visit. The Joan rested in the morning and we started the fluids early so she could have maximum energy for the social event of the day. And not to disappoint, The Joan continued to try to pawn off her jewelry and other wares to the ladies, and admittedly, I did mention to the group that there were several items for sale (which explains why Jimmy Laudeman of Pennsylvania calls me "Little Joanie"). Listen, I am only trying to help The Joan with her to-do list.

We had a lovely visit and lunched on my crowd-pleasing Chicken Parmesan on the back porch watching all our little deer, squirrels, birds, etc., eat the two tons of food delivered in their yard on a daily basis.

I realize that I am a veterinarian but we are all lifelong learners, right? My burning question is this: How does wildlife survive beyond a one-mile radius of 107 Main??? I know I've seen birds as far away as Manhattan and I can't figure it out! The collective creatures in our yard do not miss a meal that cost money! I mean it—if that bird feeder gets low on the mixed seeds, Serge or Ra are instructed (remember, I don't open the door while it's below seventy degrees) to fill the feeder, lard, throw apples for the deer, peanuts for the squirrels, etc.

The squirrels actually crawl up the deck steps and across the porch to look for their food source, i.e., The Joan. I swear I saw a squirrel cup his little hands over his eyes to look through the sliding glass doors for her, and knock! I can't be absolutely sure because I wasn't wearing my glasses but I think I saw him shake his fist when he didn't see her. And furthermore, I think that when those squirrels do see her, her head is the shape of a peanut and you can't convince me otherwise.

JOANIE'S PEARL
"Ladies should wear hats in church."

Much, much love...

* * *

NY Times correction section:
Correction for TJC#17: The Joan does not like the address 107 Main. She is fine with the "107" part but she feels the address should have been "107 Columbia Hill," and she is harboring resentment towards whoever made that very bad decision. To add to that, Serge doesn't like it at all!

He prefers the "third house on the left" approach. Ra says he's not a fan either. So I stand (alone) corrected: I am the only one who thinks "107 Main" is super cool.

* * *

Tuesday, March 13, 2012 5:34 PM
TJC #19

Hello Joanie Fans,

Yesterday was an action-packed day as we left for NY at 9:30 in the morning to make the noon pre-appointment with The Joan's oncologist. Unfortunately or fortunately he is in demand and we didn't actually see him until 2:30 PM. He did approve increasing her IV fluids to resolve the dehydration and extreme thirst, as well as increasing the dose for the fentanyl pain patch.

Remember, we have tried to make The Joan a morphine addict but she is resisting because she doesn't want to feel "dopey," especially when entertaining her fans. I'm hoping between increasing the fentanyl patch and using the Gas X (that Roy prescribed) The Joan will be more comfortable. So far, the Gas X is the hands-down winner.

But most importantly, I have to tell you how God continues to provide entertaining material for The Joan Chronicles: The Joan's sweater (pale green) matched the exam table in the doctor's office (pale green) exactly! I actually lost her for a second because she blended in so perfectly. I can't make this stuff up and Serge is my eyewitness.

Speaking of making stuff up, some of you—who shall be nameless—have questioned the truthfulness of certain items in the chronicles. My good friend Donna Butler actually marched into the house recently, with barely a salutation, only to open the refrigerator door and exclaim: "It IS true! Everything IS labeled!" Really? Do you think I actually have time to make this stuff up? I am simply observing/documenting actual events for you.

Anyway, after the two-hour delay, we experienced another two-and-a-half hour delay for the chemo, which didn't start until 5 PM. The Joan was given intravenous Benadryl which explains why she started to fall asleep in her mango Haagen Dazs sorbet. She was also given a steroid to make sure she did not have an allergic reaction to the chemo. The chemo took about an hour total so we didn't get home to start her four-hour IV fluids until 8:30 PM, which is my very long-winded explanation and excuse for not sending TJC yesterday. Phew.

Anyway, more entertainment was provided for TJC with The Joan's questions for the doctor:

1) "Can I drink wine?"
2) "Can I drink highballs?"

Which led to my questions for The Joan:

1) "Who are you?"
2) "What have you done with my mother?"

In the forty-seven years and nine months that I have personally known The Joan, I watched her have an allergic reaction after a glass of wine and swear off the stuff, but I have never, ever seen a highball touch those lips. It's true, wonders never cease (PS: The answer was "Yes... you can have it all, just don't clamp the G-tube so it goes directly into the bag.")

JOANIE'S PEARL

"If you leave bananas in the plastic bag they come in, they won't ripen too fast. On the other hand, if you need an avocado to ripen quickly, immerse it in flour and put it on top of the refrigerator."

Much, much love...

* * *

Wednesday, March 14, 2012 8:06 PM
TJC #20

Hi Everyone,

Today The Joan was down for the count. She decided that she would stay in bed because she was too tired/weak to get dressed and come downstairs. Sworn to secrecy, I wasn't permitted to tell her about her big surprise today: Kevin Cloonan from Jekyll Island! She covered herself with a sheet when he arrived, mortified that she was still in bed. (It was only her second day in bed since being sick.)

He was surprised to find her in a rose sweater, rose colored sheets and a rose cap without even knowing she would be entertaining, AND he brought a card in a rose colored envelope. God continues to work in mysterious ways. Kevin also could not restrain himself and did confirm that yes, everything in the refrigerator is labeled and most of it with a sticker that says "Joanie only."

Because The Joan was very weak, she couldn't get in many calories today. Her intravenous fluids were increased from one liter to one-and-a-half liters, but she still felt very thirsty. In a state of frustration and creativity, she said the only thing that could truly and definitively quench her thirst was... a beer! (and she did not even know about yesterday's chronicles!) I pondered the situation.

"Well," I reasoned to myself as her nutritional advisor, "Her doctor said she could have wine (12% alcohol), and whiskey (40% alcohol), so what's a little hops at 6%?" She hadn't had a morphine dose in four hours and I would make sure the tube was not clamped, so okie dokie, the vet gave the green light!

Now to the specifics. There was exactly one twelve-ounce bottle of beer in the house and it was a Beck's. No, that would not do. I asked The Joan what kind of brewski she wanted to quench her thirst, and we would get it for her. Her response: Yuengling Black and Tan from America's Oldest Brewery in Pottsville, Pennsylvania, just a holler from The Joan's birthplace! You can take the girl out of Pennsylvania... So badda-bing, badda-boom, Serge went to the beer store and returned in minutes with the liquid gold.

The Joan said she just needed a sip but I noticed half the bottle was gone in a flash and I didn't see any spilled on the bedside table either. The moral of the story is that The Joan said the beer decreased her pain and made her sleepier than morphine, so it is now her drug of choice just before bed. Plus she said it was reeeally good.

I think tomorrow will be a better day and she should still be on a sugar high after the two orange creamsicles she had after the beer. Calories are calories, people—we take what we can get... or rather we feed what will be eaten and not get stuck.

Sara Pizano, MA, DVM

JOANIE'S PEARL
"Shop for Christmas presents all year long so you can find exactly the right and special gift for your loved ones and get a good price to boot!"

With love, xo...

* * *

Thursday, March 15, 2012 7:17 PM
TJC #21

Hello Dear Loved Ones,
The Joan had a much better day today. Thank you, Mr. Yuengling! She got dressed and spent the day downstairs with Kevin and Aunt Zizi and she has been snacking on her high powered/high protein delights all day. She is also finding plenty of energy to worry about everyone else. So let's review some cutting edge treatments we have found useful on this journey we'd rather not be taking:
1) The Joan told her oncologist that she believed her hearing was decreasing as a result of the chemo treatments. She had swallowed hard several times and chewed gum and still wasn't able to hear as acutely as she had been able to, so it was clearly not that her ears needed to "pop." A hearing test was ordered and the result was the same as the first one a few years ago: normal. While driving home that day over Bear Mountain, her ears popped and she could hear normally. The Lesson: for chemo-induced hearing loss, drive up and over Bear Mountain.
2) After a fentanyl pain patch and multiple doses of morphine that many normal people become addicted to, The Joan tried Gas X at the recommendation of "Dr." Roy, the engineer, and her pain diminished greatly. The Lesson: Don't ever underestimate the amount of pain trapped gas in your intestines can cause, and Gas X works!
3) After chugging beer since yesterday afternoon through lunch today (it's 5 o'clock somewhere), The Joan has declared that Yuengling beer has provided consistent pain relief far more effective than morphine ever did, and overall she has been much more comfortable since this discovery. The Lesson: Drink alcohol regardless of your physical ailments.

So there you go, just a few more holistic recommendations we will be sharing with Sloan-Kettering, because I am sad to say that I did not see these items listed on any of their specialized menu or treatment recommendations.

JOANIE'S PEARL

"You must floss and brush your teeth when you get out of bed each morning and before you eat your breakfast lest you swallow all kinds of dangerous bacteria that have sequestered in your mouth overnight."

Xo...

* * *

Saturday, March 17, 2012 7:24 PM
TJC #22

Hello Dear Friends and Family,
Happy St. Patrick's Day! Next to Christmas, this is The Joan's favorite religious holiday so did you really have to ask what color she is wearing today? Seeing that The Joan does have Irish blood in her (that cannot be confirmed by anyone else in the family, but be that as it may) and even though we really appreciate all that the Yuengling family has done for our family, we did have to switch to Guinness, figuring it would be sacrilegious to drink anything else today.
The Joan's question for me (because I am a veterinarian) is how long she has to wait after drinking the Guinness and before taking morphine. Not being able to find that answer in my old Cornell notes or on the Addicts Anonymous website, I answered logically and said that I didn't think it was a big deal to have a little snip of beer (like the two tablespoons I thought she was planning on) with morphine, especially since her clamp would be open anyway and it would be going out of her body and into the bag. Her smile indicated that she was planning on chugging the <u>whole</u> bottle to honor the saint. So I have no choice but to resign as The Joan's veterinarian. I can no longer be held responsible for The Joan's addiction interactions—drug, alcohol or otherwise.

The last 24 hours have been relatively good. The Joan got some rad sun on her face while relaxing on the front porch and had a much needed quiet day. She's very tired and loses steam early but the pain has been fairly manageable. The prior 24 hours were not so good and she needed morphine and Ativan at regular intervals to supplement the hops and Gas X.

Now, before I tell you the rest about yesterday, I do have to warn you—it's very Adams Family. Let me remind you that the Joan's grandfather was a mortician, as was her father, uncle, brother-in-law and now nephew, Mark. So it's the norm to discuss topics around death/dying/dead bodies/viewings/funerals/plots, etc. in our family. Creepy as it may seem, yes, we all grew up around dead people and I personally played at my aunt's feet while she put make-up on that day's body in an attempt to make them look un-dead.

However, and I mean a HUGE however, it is very different talking about such things when you are talking about a person you love. The family business is the family business but the family is the family, you know?

Before Cousin Mark and family were to visit, I was instructed by The Joan to relay detailed instructions/plans/crowd control/menu options for the "after party," etc., and like a respectful daughter, did so in an email to Cousin Mark (you remember him—the good Catholic boy).

The instructions included the request to bring the casket catalog (yes, that really does exist). After a nice lunch, The Joan leafed through said catalog and if you were eavesdropping you would have sworn she was choosing a sweater from J. Crew. Comments included:

"Is this velvet or crepe?"

"But what shade of beige is this? It's hard to tell from the picture."

"This is nice detail."

"Ra, what do you think about this one?"

"Do you think this will clash with the orchid outfit I chose?"

I know, I know, you don't believe me, but I double-pinky-swear that I am quoting exact words! Again, I am the historian. I am the reporter, like Jane Pauly, simply documenting these events for you. (If anyone would like to be taken off the list at this point, I will totally understand—no hard feelings.)

Anyway, the rest of the conversation included music choices, hotel accommodations for guests and much time spent on the menu at the "after party." Please have no fear—you will not be served a normal, crappy salad, you will have several dessert choices (one of them may be cheesecake, but that has not been triple confirmed yet) and... this one is the most important... there are to be NO canned peas, period. She made Mark Boy Scout swear... that was a big one.

We laugh about it now but it wouldn't be fair if I didn't tell you that I cried the entire time. The Joan seemed to be the only one completely comfortable discussing "The Event" planning. Everyone else was just trying to stuff their hearts back into their chest. And PS, Mark assured her that all the hues of orchid would be different enough so they would coordinate and not clash. Phew. I couldn't take looking at fabric samples— that would no doubt force me to dip into the morphine elixir.

JOANIE'S PEARL
"Everyone is Irish on St. Patrick's Day!" (You saw that one coming!)

Much Love...

* * *

As hard as it was to discuss funeral arrangements, it really did make it more bearable for us to have my mom plan everything, and I really appreciated it when the time came. She intentionally planned all the details so that we wouldn't have to, because she knew how hard it would be for all of us.

It also took away any of the questions I see families debating about regarding what a loved one would want. Many times it causes problems and arguments between family members who are only trying to honor their loved ones but have disagreements about how to do that. It can tear a family apart.

You are blessing those you love when you document what you want to happen after you pass on, how you want your assets divided, your end of life wishes should you be unable to make decisions and even the funeral arrangements. But that's really the most you can do.

If families then chose to bicker and disagree after you pass, that's their sad choice.

My mom was also very conscious of her physical dependency on us and tried to stay as strong as possible to ease our "burden," for lack of a better word. That would be my definition of unselfish.

CHAPTER 9

Sunday, March 18, 2012 8:58 PM
TJC #23

To The Joan's Collection,

The Joan was very tired and weak today (she calls it "lazy" so that's the term we will use from now on), so decided to have a "snow day" and stay in bed even though it was 72 degrees (thanks be to God on the heat wave thing).

Roy flew in last night so she had his good company this morning and they yapped endlessly about who-knows-what. She wasn't able to eat tons today but I did make a good case for a new recipe that I got into her this evening: Homemade chicken/good for the soul soup puree with some mashed potatoes snuck in for kicks (but don't worry, I picked out all the frozen peas before the blender stage). Lots of butter and protein powder always make this dish a winner, so once The Joan approved, the container was slapped with a "Do not touch under penalty of law" sign. But please do not feel bad for the rest of this family... remember, I lifted the ban on the mac and cheese so they are not suffering from lack of calories. I lift bans when and only if appropriate.

The other less negative thing (if there is such a thing) about The Joan staying in bed today is that I have been in purposeful training for the last three weeks or so.

Side Bar: Several years ago, The Joan had a cardiac catheter procedure and was not able to go up and down the stairs for about five days. No problem, or so I thought, I'll come home and care for her and make sure she gets her Wheaties on time. Well, I am embarrassed to say *(having been an elite athlete a mere 30 years ago), after two days I had shin splints so severe I could hardly walk!*

Look people, there are no stairs in Florida! And, if there are stairs, they are no taller than two inches and more likely ramps. Floridians are also very fond of elevators and escalators. The stairs at 107 Main (and no mind if I have to go to the cellar or attic for something—Heaven help us, like Nana would say) are a full eight inches!!! I measured.... they are eight inches, for crying out loud!!! So now, I just pretend like I am in training for the Olympics and when she protests my going up or down <u>again,</u> I remind her it's much cheaper than a gym membership.

But The Joan, being the technical wizard that she is, was fully prepared this morning. I was in the kitchen creating some sort of masterpiece to take to her when the house phone rang. Oh boy, I thought, I better pick that up right quick in case The Joan was dozing. So imagine my surprise when it <u>was</u> The Joan on the other end of the phone calling from her cell phone: "I think I'll have my tea now... and maybe a muffin."

JOANIE'S PEARL

"When using a thermos for hot liquids, you have to pour hot water in the thermos first to heat it up. Then you can pour the water out and add your hot liquid of choice that will then stay hot."

With Love...

* * *

Monday, March 19, 2012 10:54 PM
TJC #24

Hello Family and Friends!

The Joan had a pretty tough day today. She was able to get out of bed and get dressed, but really lost steam early afternoon. She had to take a morphine dose that thankfully helped her go to la-la land for several hours and when she woke up had her dinner of puree of chicken soup (with protein powder, of course), a banana muffin straight from the oven with butter and whipped cream (with protein powder, of course), and fake coffee (with protein powder, of course). Calories are super important as this morning she was 91.2 pounds.

Another one of The Joan's recent cravings is coffee. The other day she had three caffeinated cups and then wondered why she couldn't sleep that night! Oops. So off to the health food store Roy and I went and purchased "Pero" (not to be confused with a Latino dog). It's made of exactly barley, malted barley, chicory and rye—that's it! And lo and behold that stuff sort-of-kind-of tastes like coffee and is really tasty. I tried to trick Serge and tell him I made him coffee (he loves my coffee) but he saw the can and my cover was blown. Come to think of it Serge likes anything I make! He's an easy sell and just a joy to cook for. I could put chocolate on a piece of cardboard and I think he would be delighted.

After dinner we watched the "Dancing with the Stars" premiere and I am not certain how The Joan pulled it off, but she managed to critique the entire show while semi-sleeping. I would hear her say something like: "That dress is too old for her," but when I looked at her, both eyes were closed! Amazing. More on that tomorrow with fancy pictures (remember, Roy is here) but good night for now—that premiere wore me out!

JOANIE'S PEARL

"Never sit in the back seat of a two-door car. In case of emergency, you won't be able to escape."

With love...

CHAPTER 10

Saniye Gungor and Ivan Rivas moved to Hurleyville in 2002 after purchasing a home down the road from 107 Main. Ivan is gifted at massage and shiatsu and I can tell you after a session with him, you can barely walk, you are so relaxed. And oh yes, he is also an engineer in his spare time! Saniye was a specialist in massage and medical facials for dermatologic problems. She worked with a world-renowned plastic surgeon but started to realize that so much more could be done to prevent problems with a holistic approach.

In 2005, together they opened Sanivan Holistic Retreat and Spa in the house that just so happened to have an indoor pool built by the previous owners. Besides spa treatments of all sorts, they do tailored juicing for guests and intensive detoxifications. Saniye is also an amazing raw foods and organic cuisine chef. My only complaint about her is that she never measures or remembers what amounts she used in a dish so my pleas for her to write a cookbook will seemingly go unanswered! But she did manage to give me an outline for a delicious Vegan Eggplant "Parmesan" dish that did end up being spectacular.

So all in all, Saniye and Ivan are The Joan's dream couple in the dream location, so of course, they would become *compadres*. But alas, The Joan did not even know of them until she heard someone mention something about a spa in Hurleyville at the post office in 2007. She immediately sent Sergie to investigate.

One day, he rang the doorbell at the *Sanivan Holistic Retreat and Spa* and asked, "Is this a spa?" (since there was no sign) and as Saniye says, "The rest is history." The Joan found her kindred spirits right down the street. Missing Japan and her famed Shiatsu instructor terribly, she claimed Ivan was better than any other she had ever met. That was an amazing compliment for Ivan. There are few people who know which buttons to push on which meridians to render you a wet noodle, and Ivan is one of them.

When a loved one becomes ill, we sometimes feel useless, like there is nothing we can do to help. But I promise you, even if you are just present, you will be a gift (pun intended). If you should have special talents, hobbies or just things you like to do, there are many ways you can help your loved one through this difficult time. Maybe you are an avid reader. You can read to your loved one to help pass the time. Maybe you like to play cards, you can do that with your loved one. The list is endless but the point simple. There is *always* something you can do to help, even if it's just showing up to bear witness.

Saniye chose to use her gift of massage and healing to help my mom. Once a week, she came to our home and gave my mom a massage. And it was a blessing for everyone because the more comfortable your loved one can be during this transition to Heaven, the better. But like I said, if you don't happen to be a masseuse, just being a good friend works wonders too.

* * *

Tuesday, March 20, 2012 8:49 PM
TJC #25

Dearest Loved Ones,

Well, I am happy to report that all that "laziness" yesterday paid off. I may be slipping The Joan more morphine mid-day so she can snooze and catch up. Just kidding, I would always be up front and tell her after I did it.

I think I was telling you how thirsty she's been and I've been telling her that it's because she's dehydrated and can't make up for it by drinking orally. Her doctor (her other doctor, besides me) said we could increase to two liters from one liter intravenously but The Joan was fighting me on that one. I managed to convince her to let me add another 500 cc and then yesterday (while she was sleeping) another 250. Well, what do you know? The Joan said, with astonishment, "You know, it's funny, I don't feel thirsty anymore!"

Reeeally? That's just amazing...what a mystery.

The Joan had a banner day today. Not only did she not take morphine but there was no Yuengling on the menu either! Wow! She clamped the G-tube longer today than any other day so far and she was a busy bee organizing, separating and then she organized and separated some more tchotchkes and heirlooms after that.

My mom and I are also avid recyclers so if you visit, you are expected to take at least three "Oprah" magazines and two "Prevention" magazines. We will provide a box or bag for you.

She did not snooze today but her good friend Saniye came over and gave her a massage. She must have hit some energy spots because after that (when I would need to sleep), The Joan did some more organizing and separating! I don't know about her but I'm ready for bed.

So anyway, I told you I would provide a picture/story this evening about an incident that happened yesterday. If you recall from the archives, in The Joan Chronicles #23 I told you that The Joan was analyzing "Dancing with the Stars" (DWTS) with her eyes closed. Hey, wait a minute: Very, very important sidebar: Anyone who knows me, knows that my next career goal is to be a contestant on DWTS but I also would take a close second; i.e. free tickets to the show. So last night while watching the premiere of DWTS, The Joan throws out, nonchalantly I might add, that she sold vitamins to Gavin Degraw's mother!!! Since I'm sure you were all spellbound by the show and watched it last night with bated breath, you know that Gavin was a contestant! And not only does The Joan have the mother connection, she then tells me that the mother was Rose Spada's landlord!? WHAT? Hellloooo! Rose/The Joan: Where are my backstage passes?? I checked the mail twice today and didn't see them... yet.

Anywho, back to the original story from paragraph three.... The Joan was in her morphine-induced "rest" (remember, never "sleeping") and she did it again! The living room was fairly dark—I thought she was "resting" since her eyes were closed, and I heard her cursing like a sailor! She said, "They didn't close that d#%$m cellar door AGAIN!" Poor Joanie. She can't help herself. I'm counseling her about "letting it go." So after you pick your "Oprah" magazines and "Preventions," can you please shut the cellar door on the way out?
Thanks from The Joan.

The basement door left open again!

JOANIE'S PEARL

"There should always be two dish towels in your kitchen. One for drying the dishes only, and one for drying your hands only."

With Love...

* * *

Wednesday, March 21, 2012 8:18 PM
TJC #26

Hellooooo Joanie Fans!

Another pretty good day today with plenty of projects completed and continuing organization of significant and sentimental items. The Joan's pain was intermittent and not as severe today, thankfully, but she did struggle with being nauseated. Unfortunately, she fights me on the medication for that too (Ativan) because she doesn't want to be "dopey." Today, with her oncologist's prescription, we tried a drug called Zofran instead and it didn't seem to make her drowsy. That was good since she needed it twice today. She also found comfort in the fact that our precious cat, Sebastian, was on the same medication recently for his chronic vomiting problem.

Father Lynch, The Joan's priest, came by to give her communion and hear confession. The poor soul also got some pointers from The Joan about increasing the number and involvement of congregants at his church, which I am sure he thoroughly appreciated and will discuss with his Board of Directors. We'll be watching for the Woodburne church to hit the top 10 largest in the county, just behind Joel Osteen.

And please stand by and pray for my safety. I printed all The Joan Chronicles and copy/pasted your emails (which I have read to her on a regular basis) and put them in a nice notebook for The Joan. I think the last one she read may have been number 10 and she chastised me for that one, so watch out—she says she's reading it cover to cover tomorrow and nobody is to interrupt her! Yikes! I may have an emergency nail appointment first thing.

JOANIE'S PEARL
"When cooking fish, light a smelly candle or burn incense while cooking and your kitchen/house won't stink after dinner."

Much Love...

* * *

Thursday, March 22, 2012 9:06 PM
TJC #27

Hello Dear Loved Ones,
Today our Cousin Thierry visited straight from his trip to Panama! He wanted to see The Joan for himself and give her a smooch, so when arriving in Atlanta (where he lives), instead of going home, he stayed on the plane and ended up in Hurleyville with his mom and my godmother, Zizi.

The Joan was really happy to see them, and not wanting to miss a party, struggled to stay awake. She fell asleep in the middle of the visit. Thierry and his amazing wife, Lisa, also surprised us this past Christmas Day—drove straight from Atlanta and showed up for dinner! It was a great holiday and wonderful surprise for all of us. What an amazing gift they gave my mom.

The nausea continues to be a problem but the new vice is now Haagen Dazs milk shakes with a super high calorie drink mixed in to smooth it out because the ice cream itself doesn't have enough calories—ha! And of course, no meal for The Joan would be complete without the high protein powder. (Did you have to ask?)

We seem to be done with the Yuengling for now so that will be served to you when you visit, or sent with you on your way out with your "Oprah" and "Prevention" magazines. I think the cravings are a result of not being able to absorb enough nutrients and today's included potato chips and tortilla chips—whatever The Joan wants, The Joan gets.

I think she's also a little more comfortable now because of the increase in intravenous fluids—she's up to two full liters a day and they have electrolytes added as well. When you are dehydrated it makes you feel super thirsty, tired and weak. It can also make the spasms in her intestines worse.

Oh yeah... The Joan only got up to TJC #11 today so I have a little bit of a reprieve. I can already warn you there will be several more NY Times corrections to come and likely some addendums to previous Pearls. I have also noticed a trend with The Joan... she'll say something to me and then in an afterthought instruct: "And don't put _that_ in the chronicles!" But you know, sometimes I might forget those detailed instructions; there is only so much I can fit in my little brain.

JOANIE'S PEARL

"Females should not wear underwear to bed. It's healthy for their bodies to air out."

With Love and a PS: I can't resist telling you that when Isabel (Zizi's granddaughter, Cat's daughter and Thierry's niece) was about six years old, her mom was getting her ready for bed after a visit at Aunt Joan's and Grandpa-Uncle Serge's, and when Cat went to put her underwear on *she announced in a panic: "But Aunt Joan said it's not healthy for girls to wear underwear to bed! Our bodies need to breathe!"*

* * *

Friday, March 23, 2012 9:55 PM
TJC #28

Helllllloooooo Joanie Fans,

Last night was rough for The Joan, with lots of pain, so she did have to take morphine. She woke up very "lazy" but still had to be strongly encouraged to stay in bed. I reminded her that today was National Wear Your Pajamas To Work Day (if not today, it was sometime this week—seriously—so that would explain why some of you may have seen your Bank of America teller in flannels), but The Joan was not impressed by another Hallmark holiday. In bed today, though, she did have time to finish The Joan Chronicles, up to #22...yikes! I also copied and pasted many of your emails in chronological order for a total of 104 pages so far! I am thankful to report that I am still here, the locks have not been changed and I interpret that as a good sign for my future wellbeing.

The Joan struggled with being nauseous today and was sick this morning, which is not good since it throws off the baby bird eating schedule, and nutrition is so vital at this point. Thankfully, The Joan got a little bit of a second wind at 6 PM and came downstairs to finish organizing the coffee table (both levels), and down the Haagen Dasz shake which outbid the Yuengling again. (However, it was a close tossup and we may be back to hard alcohol soon, who knows what tomorrow will bring.)

The Joan was also sad this morning since Roy flew back to Miami and she said it feels weird that he's not here. I'm having him research moving our three horses, three cats, Jack Russell and his business to Hurleyville but strangely he didn't seem too enthusiastic about that prospect. I'm all for it until winter settles in here around August 1.

JOANIE'S PEARL
"Curtains trap a lot of dust and dirt so when spring cleaning, do all the cleaning and dusting (with the windows open) while

the curtains and drapes are being washed, so they are put back into a clean environment."

With Love and another PS: Don't forget to call Sergie on Sunday to say Happy 79th Birthday!

* * *

Saturday, March 24, 2012 5:52 PM
TJC #29

Hi Everyone,

The Joan felt so good this morning that we actually talked about going for a Sunday drive (yes, I realize it's Saturday but we disregard all time zones). We didn't end up going for a ride but I think it was a positive thing to talk about in any case.

And The Joan was pain free today until a few minutes ago and after the Dunkin' Donuts Boston Cream (the one with the powdered sugar and not the chocolate) and the tiny glass of Lactaid. The Boston Cream, in any event, will be off the menu and the process of elimination continues.

The Joan also felt good enough to trek to the basement where she swore she had a cheesecake pan—the one that I could not locate. Sergie requested Cousin Michelle's cheesecake with the cherries on top for his birthday cake so... down we went. Since she was already hooked up to her intravenous fluids I had to be the IV pole. Have any of you ever had to "be" the IV pole? Like maybe in your 5th grade play? It's not as easy as it looks, I will tell you that. Remember, my lower body is getting in shape because of the stairs that, you will recall, are freakishly high here at 107 Main.

(*Sidebar question: When The Joan once wore a pedometer, how many steps did she walk <u>inside</u> the house in <u>one</u> day? See answer at bottom of TJC #29.)

Anywho, being the IV pole requires advanced upper body strength and admittedly, I had to rest against a pole several times and change arms frequently. Confident that the pan was not where she left it last, I was resigned to using all different shapes of pans and cannot be held responsible if the middle of the cheesecake is not done. I am not sure how much jiggle is the right amount so Sergie may be having a cheesecake shake with a floating candle in it whilst we sing "Happy Birthday." It could be worse.

And I just wanted to take a minute and thank everyone for loving The Joan so much. Thank you to Carolyn for the beautiful Japanese arrangement, to Sylviette for the gorgeous orchids, the Harmins for the pretty bouquet, Aunt Zizi for the potted plants and all your calls, emails and cards. We really appreciate it, and I am sorry if I forgot anyone, but thank you too!

JOANIE'S PEARL
"When you start a project, finish it!"

Much Love...

*Sidebar answer: 10,000 steps!

* * *

Sunday, March 25, 2012 8:13 PM
TJC #30

To our Dearest Dearest,

The Joan started off slow today and had a lazy morning in bed, resting before Sergie's birthday lunch party. Susan made a beautiful meal for us (thank you, Susan!) that we enjoyed with Sue, Ken and my friend and old college roommate, Donna Butler.

Donna was passing by between Syracuse and NJ and loves the Pizanos. The Joan thinks that Donna is actually her daughter instead of me (a switched-at-birth type of thing that she cannot thoroughly explain) because she is more like The Joan than I am. Today, I thought maybe my parents really are her parents because after she had Susan's delicious lunch <u>and</u> a generous helping of Sergie's birthday cherry cheesecake (that was cooked to perfection and Sergie loved!) Donna asked, "Didn't you mention there were <u>two</u> desserts?"

Does that sound like Sergie or what?! Mmmmm... coincidence? Not only that, she arrived with chocolate covered pretzels and fancy coffee for his birthday celebration—both Sergie's faves—without any coaching!

The Joan feels like she needs to get more exercise so decided it was a good time to inspect the grounds. It was a beautiful day so off we went en masse. And, see that—Sergie got to be the IV pole! And then Donna got to be the IV pole!

Joan, Serge (being the IV pole), me and Donna Butler inspecting the estate

If you plan to visit, you may want to work your upper body first in case you are called upon to rotate in as The Joan may be on the brink of gardening. I will warn you that if you are going to be the IV pole, it's no joke and you have to pay close attention—The Joan is quick.

She picked some of our beautiful daffodils in full bloom along the house and spent some time this afternoon basking in the sun. And then... bam... The Spirit of Spring Break hit her! (No doubt from the warmth of the sun and smell of Hawaiian Tropic sunscreen.) "I'll have a beer," she announced. Phew—it's a good thing I didn't pass them out with the "Oprah" and "Prevention" magazines when I thought we were over that craving—lesson learned and mental note: donuts off/beer on.

Well, dear ones, now I have a teeny weeny sort of confession to make: so far I have paraphrased Joanie's Pearls (you probably guessed that when you read the one about "flooring it" out of the driveway). Mind you, they are all true Pearls and all The Joan's, but now that she has read the chronicles up to TJC #18, she has decided she is feeding me the Pearls. So here goes and she says to tell you this is a very important one:

JOANIE'S PEARL
"During warm weather, place full screens in your windows. That way, you can keep the top part open so the hot air will go out and keep the room cool." *(See Joanie's Pearls/TJC #9 about the heat going out the top of your head—same principle applies)*

Much love...

* * *

Monday, March 26, 2012 7:44 PM
TJC #31

Helll...lllll....oooo (teeth chattering),
Mother Nature is playing a cruel, cruel joke on us here in Hurleyville—it's freezing again! The Joan was always fine with 36-degree temperatures (and that was inside the house... ba-da-boom) and even now with very little body fat, the cold doesn't bother her like it freezes my blood. I was telling my cousin that the other day that I was wearing a turtle neck sweater. I then put my fleece jacket on and zipped it to my chin, and The Joan asked me where I was going. I said "Upstairs." Remember, there is no heat to rise in this house and the power of the space heater from the back porch doesn't cut it.
*Anyway, today was a monumental day, in fact, miraculous. In terms of miracles I would say right between the parting of the Red Sea and when Jesus turned water into wine (with the vino being the coolest). It's that something I am not allowed to come right out and say but you will remember it was "Hurdle **Number 2**" in a previous chronicle and it hasn't occurred since Sunday, March 4. Fabulous, fabulous news and a true blessing!*
The Joan was up and dressed early this morning—8:30 AM! That's two-and-a-half hours ahead of schedule, which explains why she is going to bed now at 7:42! She's been pretty much pain-free with minor and intermittent spasms and is now attributing this to my fabulous menu/diet that I mush for her and pretty much serve in a consistency that won't clog the G-tube or her small and large intestines.
The Joan is afraid to clog the G-tube mostly because the nurse at Sloan told her if it really gets impacted she should use Coca Cola to

dissolve the clog, and The Joan flatly refuses to put a substance into her body that would act like Drano and takes rust off pennies. That one scared her into submission. So overall, I would say a great day and The Joan had a restful and peaceful one, thank goodness.

Lastly, thank you to Kevin for reminding me about this next Pearl:

JOANIE'S PEARL

"When you get in the pool to cool off, you have to stay in long enough for your insides to cool down or you won't feel refreshed when you get out."

Much love and peace...

* * *

Tuesday, March 27, 2012 8:59 PM
TJC #32

Joanie having a very bad night—severe pain and nausea. Waiting for drugs to kick in—will update you tomorrow.

Much Love...

* * *

Wednesday, March 28, 2012 9:26 AM
TJC #33

Good Morning Loved Ones,

First and most important, The Joan is feeling pretty good this morning! So now I will tell you about yesterday. I've been saying The Joan has good days and bad days but it's more like good hours and bad hours. Typically, she is strongest between 11 AM and say, 2 PM. After that, she gets very tired and often nauseous. It seems most evenings are the hardest, so the days are a little bit of a rollercoaster.

Yesterday she was feeling nauseous in the afternoon and the first medication didn't help, so she took the second medication (that can be taken together). She became progressively more painful and by the evening was in severe discomfort, so took morphine. With any pain medication (and this goes for dogs and cats too, for all you pet owners), they work best as a preventative, as opposed to when the pain is severe.

But, alas, The Joan is resisting taking morphine during the day because she doesn't want to be dopey or fall asleep during the day and not be able to (1) sleep at night or (2) entertain guests. I realize the Ad Council spent millions on their "Say NO to drugs" campaign, but please encourage The Joan to "Say YES to drugs." I'll make you some bumper stickers and T-shirts. We have asked the doctor for an alternative but he continues to say "morphine is the best." Sad commentary on the drug industry because "the best" is not working.

So after she took the two drugs for nausea, she took Gas X, currently the most effective drug in our arsenal (never underestimate the pain that trapped air can cause you) and then finally morphine. The other thing that helped was my tried-and-true Linus blanket—the heating pad. Love the heating pad. She drifted off to sleep for a few minutes on the back porch and then decided she could make it to bed. Ra and Serge helped her get up in her drugged stupor. She stood up and said (you won't be surprised), "This place is a mess!" And then she attempted to tidy up.

Really? Do we really have to worry about the crossword puzzle book on the table right now? Methinks we have more important things to worry about, eh? So off she went to bed and slept well (thanks to saying YES to drugs) and is now dressed and downstairs. We continue to look for the exit sign off this crazy rollercoaster.

JOANIE'S PEARL
"Wallpaper never goes out of style."

Much Love...

* * *

Thursday, March 29, 2012 7:04 PM
TJC #34

Dear Friends, Family and Fans,
The Joan is doing well today, and hasn't needed morphine since Tuesday night—the really bad, bad night. The Yuengling yesterday and

today may have something to do with that but I cannot scientifically state that; it's simply anecdotal. To date, The Joan has consumed three bottles. I know you may be surprised to hear that, since I have reported many times that she's tossed a little hops back, but The Joan is nursing a beer like no other these days. Drinking one twelve-ounce bottle is a very loooong and somewhat complicated process.

First, you open the bottle and let it sit in the refrigerator because it must be very, very cold. Next, you pour a little, approximately four ounces but not anymore, in the medium glass (not the small glass and not the large glass), and it must be served with a spoon.

Then The Joan (or I) take the spoon and stir really fast to create a head of bubbles. The Joan wants just the beer, not the fizz.... no need for extra air in that gut. In the next step, the bubbles are removed or sort of held back with the spoon when she sips. Coincidentally, as I wrote this, The Joan belched really loud, like a sailor. Mental note: need to stir more next time for less effervescence.

Uncle George and Aunt Teddy visited today, hot off the road from sunny Florida, and we had a nice lunch and visit. They didn't get to see our pet deer that now visit us twice daily but we did see a newcomer in the backyard, a beautiful pheasant. I was relieved that my Uncle George wasn't packing any heat from his vast collection.

The Joan also worked on her picture board for her funeral (we will from now on refer to as "The Event") and has been doing so for several weeks. My family will not have any planning to do, we'll just have to show up and sob nonstop. The Joan is concerned however, that she may inadvertently forget someone. She's noticing she's been a little forgetful lately so I will tell her and you will promise to bring a picture of yourself to The Event she's planning so she won't feel bad, and just in case. We all know she will be there!

Many of you have emailed various questions or comments and if I think they may be helpful to the group, I'll include them in a chronicle. Today's question comes to us from Cousin Mimi:

"Dear Joanie's Pearls,

Wallpaper may never go out of style but what about borders? I have a wallpaper border in my dining room and I think it's outdated. What do you think?"

Signed,
Helpless in Horsham"

"Dear Helpless,
    The Joan feels that borders are really out of style except for very special situations like maybe a bathroom. She also wants to clarify that using wallpaper as an accent wall (Editor's note: like all designers are doing today) is distracting and unsightly.

Sincerely,
Joanie's Pearls Correspondent"

JOANIE'S PEARL
    "If you change the dirt for your daffodil bulbs once a year, they will multiply like rabbits."

With love...

* * *

Friday, March 30, 2012 8:01 PM
TJC #35

Dear Joanie's Collection,
    The Joan had a pretty good day today but again woke up very tired... I mean, lazy. Brenda Haye stopped by for a nice visit and took a stroll down the Japanese Memory Lane. Brenda was an exchange professor when The Joan and Serge were the Honorary Mayor and Mayoress of Kosugi, Japan, circa 1989-1993. And bless her heart, she says she has been trying to "get into the family ever since." Today I told her that she entered the family in the late 80s and to boot she provided two "fill in" grandchildren! What a blessing she's been.
    So The Joan has a son (Rafael) and three daughters (me, Donna Butler and Brenda Haye). The Joan always wanted six children, so only two to go. Please let me know if you would like me to forward the required paperwork.
    The Joan has kept in touch with friends in Kosugi, Japan, although her English lessons while there have not stood the test of time, so

communicating on the phone is a touch challenging. And remember, The Joan is trilingual (English/Japanese/Spanish) so when speaking on the phone last evening to her Japanese friends, she sometimes used all three languages. It did not prove an effective communication tool but it made for a good laugh (for Serge and me) while attempting to exchange email addresses. Rest assured, someone on the planet will get an email from The Joan but we can't be certain who or where. Oh well, we'll simply add them to The Collection.

Speaking of good laughs: here's another story <u>I could not possibly make up</u>. If you recall from last night's Chronicles (#34) you received directions regarding the serving of the Yuengling in the event that you are called upon to serve one to The Joan in her time of dire need and distress. I hit "send" and thought nothing of it. Might I remind you that I do not allow previews of TJC at 107 Main and I do not allow The Joan to edit anything before sending. A wise old superior of mine once told me it's always better to ask for forgiveness than permission (being my superior, he later regretted sharing that pearl with me but whatever!) Not five minutes later, The Joan asked Serge for a Yuengling. I sat back and watched it all unfold, not disclosing TJC content. Here's how it went:

"Serge?" The Joan asked.

"Yes," Serge answered.

"I would like a beer," The Joan stated and we all know now that means one-third of a beer that has been left open in the fridge for at least 24 hours.

...Pause...

"Only FOUR ounces," The Joan called out as Serge left the room.

"OK," Serge responded.

"And with a spoon!" The Joan instructed while he was walking down the stairs.

With that, I burst into fits of laughter and realized that maybe I had not completely shared all of the Standard Operating Procedures for maintaining The Joan! My bad. I referred Sergie to TJC #34 and rolled out of the room, unable to control myself. And PS, the poor dear... when he returned with the four ounces and spoon in tow, she mumbled, "Too many bubbles!" Oh boy. Have no fear, detailed training sessions are now scheduled, and attendance is mandatory.

Now today's Pearl is thanks to Brenda Haye, and needs a little 'splainin' for you to fully appreciate it. When Brenda had her first child,

The Joan was called upon to rotate in since Brenda had some surgical complications from her C-section. Not one to sit around while Brenda and the first born, Nora, were napping peacefully, The Joan set out to sterilize the house. Seeing that there was no bucket (whhaaaaat????) to clean with, The Joan had no choice but to utilize her available resources. (But don't worry, she left Brenda a list of needed cleaning supplies.) Brenda wants you to know that she utilizes this Pearl to this day, even though her daughter is now a "tween."

JOANIE'S PEARL
"Baby wipes make excellent cleaning tools for baseboards."

With Love...

* * *

Saturday, March 31, 2012 9:26 PM
TJC #36

Dearest Dearests,
The Joan had a pretty tough day today. She was very nauseous and uncomfortable this morning, so spent most of the day in bed. She was able to take her pseudo-shower (she has to be wrapped in all kinds of waterproof cellophane to cover patch, port and tube) and change nighties, and came downstairs late afternoon for her second IV bag and change of scenery.

Since January or so, her weight has dropped rapidly, but stayed in the low nineties for a few weeks now, and seems to be fairly stable. The Joan had to take both kinds of meds for the nausea a couple times today and just took morphine now. She will no doubt sleep like a log.

Still, The Joan acknowledges several benefits to being sick. Here's her Top Ten list:

10) She doesn't have to go grocery shopping, which she dislikes.
9) She doesn't have to do laundry.
8) She doesn't have to pay bills or manage household finances.
7) She gets to go to Manhattan often and occasionally catches a Broadway show.

6) *She doesn't have to shave her legs (no hair since chemo).*
5) *She can smell and taste her food after thirty years of not being able to!*
4) *Her hair temporarily grew back wavy (a long-term dream).*
3) *She is back to her "wedding weight" (a long-term goal).*
2) *She doesn't have to cook and has all her personally-designed meals served to her.*

    ...And The Joan's Number One perceived benefit to being sick (not that she would recommend it to anyone):

1) *She is surrounded by her family!*

JOANIE'S PEARL

    "After doing a load of wash, leave the top of the washing machine open to air out. This will extend the life of the washing machine."

Much Love...

* * *

Sunday, April 1, 2012 9:07 PM
TJC # 37

Dear Loved Ones,

    The Joan had a pretty good day today and was ...(drum roll)... drug and alcohol free! But even with all the extra rest yesterday, she was still pretty fatigued today. Last evening she did give me a tiny bit of a scare though.

    You know that on the pain scale you and I would say we were a "Ten" if we were in excruciating pain ("One" is not so much pain). The Joan would say "Five" for the same pain, so when she says she needs morphine it's really bad.

    The Joan is a steel tank, reinforced with steel. Last night as she was going to bed, she said to me, "I think I need to take something." My first thought was, "uh oh," because when The Joan feels awful, you feel awful. But now that I am her full time veterinarian, I've developed a knack for reading her mind or knowing what she needs before she knows it.

Anyway, my second thought was, "I know what treatment she's talking about," and asked, "Do you need a brewsky?" Phew, yes, she needed a brewsky and people, strap on your seatbelts: SIX ounces, not the four that I reported in TJC #35. This is the reason that the Standard Operating Procedures are in pencil. I have no idea when they can be printed and bound.

(Oops—did I say that? The Joan announced today: "Enough with the beer in the chronicles—you're making me sound like a lush!" Again, there is only so much I can fit in my little pea brain and I simply forgot.)

Cousins Karen and Tara came for lunch today since it has been about twenty years since their last visit. They figured it was time, and it was sooo good to see them. They were fortunate enough to coincidentally schedule during Test Recipe and Stock Up Weekend (someone may have tipped them off, but I can't be sure who). They had several menu choices that included chicken curry with spinach linguini (successful test), OR a turkey and Swiss sandwich (always in stock) with coleslaw, OR herb roasted chicken, mashed potatoes and salad (stock). This also included a hot and/or cold beverage, beer or wine at no extra charge. 107 Main is an excellent test kitchen site since Sergie eats everything (remember Mikey?) and the more stuff/sauce/spice/herbs you pile on, the better. I can even mix a few leftovers together and he thinks it's great! It's very satisfying to be the personal chef for the Pizano family—hard to go wrong. My beloved is more a Plain Jane kind of eater so there are far less ingredients in my Miami kitchen.

The Cousins also benefited from another test recipe: Pear Frangipane. The Joan had a choice of chicken soup mush, chicken mush soup or puree of chicken soup. She opted for the first and loved it and was thankfully able to enjoy the Pear Frangipane too!

JOANIE'S PEARL

"Feel free to use and enjoy your good silverware and china any day of the week—that's what it's there for!"

With Love...

* * *

Sara Pizano, MA, DVM

Monday, April 2, 2012 8:52 PM
TJC #38

Hi Everyone,
    It seems that whenever I hit "send" on a chronicle, the opposite of
what I just wrote happens. That would be good if I told you something
bad, but bad if told you something good. Get it?
    The Joan seems to be in a pattern. First thing in the morning she feels
kind of nauseous. Then her best hours are between 11 AM and 2 PM,
which is why we have established those visiting hours. At about 2 PM,
maybe 3 PM, the curtains start going down and she needs a snooze...I
mean "rest". Evenings seem to be her worst time and tonight was another
bad one. She had to take both Zofran and Ativan for the nausea and
morphine for pain.
    She had to wait it out on the back patio room and was pretty weak.
Again, though, not one to pass a chore that needs to be done and seeing
laundry on the floor, The Joan opened the cellar door. In a moment of
panic and with a spike in his normally low blood pressure, Sergie asked,
"Where are you going?!?!?" to which The Joan replied, "Downstairs," and
the Serge questioned "WHAT?" to which The Joan replied calmly/weakly
"April Fool's." The Joan is a card.
    You'll also be happy to know that The Joan is caught up on all the
chronicles and though she did debate a few Pearl points, I made my case
and have no retractions at this time. She is throwing them out there on
a regular basis now. She'll say something and then add, "And that's a
Pearl!" so stay tuned.

JOANIE'S PEARL
    "When loved ones visit from far away and are leaving,
    stand at the end of the driveway and wave until you can't see
    their car."

Much Love...

* * *

Tuesday, April 3, 2012 9:12 PM
TJC #39

Hello, Hello, Hello!

The Joan had a good day today! So good, in fact, she is planning a "lunch" outing tomorrow. "Lunch" is in quotations since it's actually just an excuse to get (probably me) out of the house and not actually to eat lunch. The Joan will be eating at 107 Main since I haven't seen any high protein, low fiber pureed items that only include overcooked beans/beets/carrots on any lunch menus lately. Also, and excuse the graphics, the "lunch" gastric bag is smaller than the "home" gastric bag and, strategically strapped to her leg under her maternity pants so as to be fashionably concealed.

The Joan will probably have some tea and tell the waitress she already ate which is why she's only ordering the Chamomile. Now, mind you, several lunch outings have been planned previously but not implemented—so fingers crossed. The plan is to hookup the IV's early, unhook, "lunch," then back to hookup and squeeze-in a total of eight hours of IV fluids. On second thought, toes crossed too.

And now, dear ones, I have to tell you that the chronicles staff (that's me) has decided to decrease the number of days the chronicles is published. For the most part, The Joan is doing really well (and don't you think that she won't be telling her oncologist that my diet works miracles!... She will no doubt have me on the Sloan Kettering lecture circuit any day... I best rest up) so I will only be sending a chronicle when we have (1) significant news (2) something funny to tell you (3) an important Pearl you can't live without.

And double Holy Cow: (4) is that last night I told you that when I tell you something, the opposite happens... and between paragraphs two and three a bad thing happened! My first line was about The Joan having a good day and then between two and three, she vomited (which she has done only one other time since home). I'm starting to worry about a poltergeist. The good news is that she said she "got it all out," so thinks she can sleep just fine. In addition, I usually vomit as an act of solidarity when someone else vomits but I didn't! Something to be proud of but still heartbreaking when someone you love is ill.

So now that we are emotionally and physically spent, I will leave you with a Pearl that my good friend Annie (oh yeah, another one of

The Joan's adopted daughters) reminded me of, and The Joan said "Of course!" (earlier today, before she got sick):

JOANIE AND ANNIE'S PEARL
"When taking one of your homemade dishes to a loved one's party, include the recipe!"

With Love and stay tuned...

* * *

Thursday, April 5, 2012 8:39 PM
TJC #40

Hi Everyone,
It's been a rocky road since the last chronicle. The Joan has been suffering with severe nausea and vomited twice. The two different drugs (Ativan and Zofran) didn't really help enough for her to eat, so we called in the big guns—no, not Mr. Yuengling... Saniye!
Saniye was nice enough to come over and do pressure points to relieve the nausea, and The Joan ended up sleeping really well. Unfortunately, she was not able to eat anything at all for over 36 hours, and today the few things she did eat created pain.
These symptoms are very bad and most likely mean that the obstructions are progressing. I spoke to the oncologist's office and requested an additional drug for the nausea called Compazine, so hopefully The Joan will use it when needed. Compazine is a very powerful anti-nausea drug but one of the side effects is drowsiness. The Joan will not be allowed to operate any heavy machinery, so rotor-tilling is out, plus we all know how The Joan feels about feeling "dopey." I can't even sneak this one to her since the route is where the sun doesn't shine, if you know what I mean. Sorry to be so graphic, but cancer is not polite.
The Joan stayed in bed under that electric blanket (remember we are still in the dead of winter here in the boonies), until about 1 PM then got dressed and came downstairs! She said she needed to get out so we took a ride to Grahamsville. This was no doubt a ploy to get me out of the house, but for crying out loud I went to Shoprite <u>and</u> Family Drug today—I can only fit so much into my busy schedule.

Anyway, I drove Miss Daisy with Sergie to Grahamsville and we stopped at a nice little bakery and specialty store for a snack. The Joan's choices were limited to baby food, apple pie (just the inside), or chicken soup (but not the chicken—too tough—see today's Pearl). The Joan selected the chicken soup and left the chicken for the resident cat. It was a beautiful ride and sunny day. So glad we were able to take a field trip.

The other thing the doctor's office said was that we could increase her morphine dose, so when she requested it tonight I told her it was OK'd by an actual oncology staff person and not just me. I think she was cursing me under her breath as her eyes started closing on the way up the stairs. The Joan is very sensitive to drugs, but someone had to do it—I don't want The Joan to be in pain!

So, dear ones, the last piece of news I have for you today is that The Joan decided to do one more chemo treatment. She is doing this in the hopes that the tumors causing the worst parts of the obstructions will at least be reduced a little so she is more comfortable. We will be going to NYC Monday morning and coming home Tuesday morning.

JOANIE'S PEARL
"After making chicken soup, keep the chicken separate in the refrigerator so it doesn't get tough sitting in the soup."

Much, much love...

* * *

Friday, April 6, 2012 9:43 PM
TJC #41

Hi Everyone,

I'm afraid that I don't have good news at the moment. The vomiting has persisted since Tuesday night and The Joan has had virtually no calories since. She was just admitted to Sloan and the x-ray shows an obstruction. She is comfortable now and getting the anti-nausea medication intravenously along with the IV fluids. Sergie went to our "city apartment," the lovely 3V, owned by our precious and exceedingly generous friends, the Dunns. Ra will be joining us in the morning.

Sara Pizano, MA, DVM

I wanted to wait a little while longer to possibly speak to the doctor tonight but he was busy in the ER and The Joan kicked me out. She was busy organizing her bedside table, walked me to the elevator to make sure I got in and then continued to wheel and deal with Joyce-the-nurse regarding the sale of some Japanese items (Joyce is scheduled to come to 107 Main to pick up the goods). Yes—that was all happening at 9:30 PM.

Also, important communication alert: We seem to have forgotten Joanie's cell in the car so Joanie has Sergie's cell. If you want to get in touch with us, emailing me is easiest, or I have my cell but please try text or email first.

Anyway, the Pearl tonight is really only for Joanie—lest you all abide by this one and all the white poodles in shelters everywhere remain homeless. There was a picture of someone's super cute little tiny white poodle in the ER tonight so:

JOANIE'S PEARL SPECIFIC FOR HER

"Adopt a beige poodle, not white, so they don't show the dirt."

I will email you all in the morning to give you another update. We don't have a plan as of yet except "nothing by mouth."

With Love and Thanks for all of yours...

* * *

Saturday, April 7, 2012 9:15 AM
TJC #42

Good Morning Loved Ones,

If you didn't already, please read TJC #41 sent late last night so you know what's going on.

This morning The Joan feels pretty good. No vomiting last night and the intravenous Zofran worked well to control her nausea. Because of all the vomiting, she has lost most of her voice. The oncology team was in this morning and their plan is as follows:

- *Nothing by mouth and if there is no more vomiting, try clear liquids tomorrow.*
- *Stay on intravenous medications for nausea, and before home will try a different one that dissolves in the mouth. (I did tell them I was her veterinarian but surprisingly they were still not willing to bend any pharmacy laws and send us home with injectable anti-nausea meds for me to give.)*
- *Try a different pain med if needed (I explained that The Joan is not a morphine fan) but none needed so far today.*
- *If she still decides to do the chemo Monday (which I think she should do as it's truly the only thing that can get to the cause and possibly shrink the tumors enough for her to be comfortable) then the best case scenario is that she would be released Monday morning and then go to the noon doctor/chemo appointment then home on Tuesday.*

The Joan's plan is as follows:

- *Do a lap around the floor every hour (started at 7 AM).*
- *Nap in between laps.*
- *10:30 AM: possibly go to woodworking in the rec room.*
- *3 PM: attend recital by Julliard students (piano and cello).*
- *Stop vomiting.*
- *Organize bedside table.*
- *Find handyman to fix remote control. (Can you believe that The Joan has never turned on the TV in the hospital in four visits but this morning, while trying to watch the Today program, the remote didn't work!!!?)*
- *Get dolled-up to see Bobby-the-Doorman who will be visiting after his shift.*

Communication Update: Sergie located The Joan's phone (left accidentally in the car) so all phones are now with their rightful owners. Unfortunately, The Joan lost her voice so talking on the phone is not an option at the moment.

Sara Pizano, MA, DVM

JOANIE'S PEARL
"Keep moving so your feet don't swell."

Much Love...

* * *

Sunday, April 8, 2012
TJC # 43

Happy Empty Tomb Day! (That's what we say at my church) and Happy Belated Pessah!

The Joan is pretty weak today and because she hasn't been as active, her feet are a little swollen with fluid (called edema). The hourly laps didn't quite pan out yesterday but she did them as often as she could. We also napped through the woodworking workshop and were double booked in the afternoon but we remain flexible with our very busy social calendar and schedule whilst at Sloan.

Bobby-the-Doorman visited after his shift, which overlapped with the Julliard concert so we missed that one but it was well worth it. The Joan did a lap with Bobby-the-Doorman, after which we heard a very informative story regarding the medical Mary Jane (not to be confused with The Joan's sister Mary Jane).

Bobby-the-Doorman said that when his cousin was ill with cancer, he rolled the ganga in his room on the second floor of his mom's house. Wishing to be discrete, he threw the seeds out the back window, where the neighbor Mayor had a direct view. Months later, the neighbor Mayor said to Bobby-the-Doorman's aunt, "What are those lovely plants you're growing in your backyard?" To which the aunt replied, "I have no idea, they just started growing but aren't they pretty?" Now before you get excited about a big harvest, that was twenty years ago and I'm not giving you the address!

Our big Easter surprise was a visit from Father Ignatius. You'll recall the Father from The Joan Chronicles #4 as the non-skiing-Doogie-Howser-look-a-like-priest! A couple Hail Marys and Our Fathers, a little bit of the communion wafer and he was off to Easter mass at his church.

The other exciting Easter news is that The Joan's roommate moved out! The rooms here are doubles unless you pay $500 clams a night for *a private—yikes. The Joan had some unfortunate experiences with TV addicted/hard of hearing roommates, so it's been hard for her to rest during past visits (and if I personally heard one more episode of The Family Feud I was going to jump out the window).*

Her latest roommate was very quiet and thankfully in the no-TV zone, but it's still nice to have a big room to ourselves. We took over and are using every piece of furniture in the room so the unlucky cleaning crew will have to Lysol again before the next roomie—sorry about that, but The Joan likes to stretch out!

The Joan is now sipping on some herb tea—the first thing by mouth in days, so we'll see how that goes. She is torn about having the chemo tomorrow and is getting worn out. Being nauseous is no fun. We've assured her that we will support any decision she makes.

Today or tomorrow we will be speaking to someone (anyone who knows) about homecare, since I believe it will be best that she receives injectable drugs for the nausea and they won't let me do that. Someone will have to figure out how to provide those services, so we'll keep you posted.

JOANIE'S PEARL
"When cooking a turkey or chicken, throw everything into an oven bag (found near the tin foil at your local grocer). There's no basting or wasting time and it comes out delicious every time."

With Love...

* * *

Monday, April 9, 2012 9:50 AM
TJC #44

Dear Loved Ones,
I am afraid that The Joan has taken a serious turn for the worse. I am so, so sorry to have to tell you what is happening. After she drank a little broth and tea, she experienced an enormous amount of pain and nausea last evening that was very difficult to control. She ended up having a comfortable night with the IV pain meds and meds for nausea and is

now being placed on a pump with that pain medication (Dilantin). An x-ray last night at 11 PM showed the same obstruction as Friday and her intestines are now totally blocked. Serge and I were here until 1 AM and Ra stayed with her the whole night.

I don't believe she will be able to eat again and once we have the pain pump set and feel it is an appropriate rate and dose to keep her pain-free, we will be going home with it under the care of Hospice. The Joan is sedate and groggy but can speak to us a little bit. Her most imperative message to me was that no matter what, I was not to change her into that ugly blue hospital gown. We all have priorities.

The oncology team was in this morning and there will be no chemo as they feel it could make the situation worse. Now we are just waiting for the caseworker to help us set up the necessary services at home. We will most likely be going home tomorrow and want you to know how much we love and appreciate all of you.

With much love and peace to you...

* * *

Monday, April 9, 2012 9:55 PM
TJC #45

Dearest Dearests,

Today, thankfully, The Joan had a pain-free day. I also wanted you to know that The Joan is still entertaining and cracking some jokes. She is now on a pump so when she feels uncomfortable she hits the pump to dispense the pain meds (up to six times an hour). This pump will go home with us and be managed by hospice and us. The unfortunate side effect for The Joan, as you well know, is sedation and she spent most of the day in bed snoozing and a little while in the chair (also snoozing).

Around 5 PM she decided she was simply annoyed with herself and complained, "I wasted a whole day!" and the sedation seemed to wear off a little bit, although she is still very, very weak. The Joan also decided it was unhealthy for her to stay in bed all day so vowed to "move more," and did a quarter-lap tonight. She is moving at a snail's pace and maybe even slower but any movement is better than staying in bed.

The plan for tomorrow is to be discharged around noon. The Joan and I will be going to 107 Main by ambulance and Sergie will be driving alone. Ra is already home preparing the house since a medical bed will be delivered this week. Placement is still under debate but I am voting to transform the sunroom into the master bedroom. The Joan is worried about "where visitors will sit"—I assured her nobody cared even if they had to sit on the floor—and Roy arrives tomorrow... YAY! Hospice will begin with us tomorrow.

The Joan also felt well enough to answer a request for a Pearl from sweet Carolina. The attached picture is quite unusual, since this baby has not stopped smiling since she exited the womb, plus she adores her cat:

"Help me grandma Joanie!!!!

I have started to eat cereal in the morning and my cat wants to eat my food! I need a Pearl for this situation!!!! She never got onto the table before, but this morning she found her way up (not an easy task as she weighs more than me). What should I do? Thanks for your advice, yours truly, Carolina."

Carolina fearing the competition with her cat over her beloved cereal

Sara Pizano, MA, DVM

Dear Carolina,
    The solution is simple. Feed your cat on the floor at the same time you are eating and you'll have the cereal all to yourself.
Love, Grandma Joanie.

The Joan is also spitting out pearls left and right. This one is compliments of The Reading School of Nursing, circa 1950:

JOANIE'S PEARL
    "The pillow cases on a hospital bed should open towards the closest wall so the inside of the pillows don't collect dust."

The Joan is tucked in for the night and resting comfortably. I hope we can all do the same.

With much love...

* * *

Tuesday, April 10, 2012 10:33 AM
TJC #46

Lots of Good News Joanie Fans!
    The Joan was switched to a constant rate infusion (CRI) of intravenous morphine, plus the ability to pump more—up to six times a day. She didn't need to pump since last evening and is much more alert and strong! She's doing her second lap now. I think she was so annoyed at how groggy the pain meds were making her that her body decided to compensate and metabolize them extra quick. Sedation is unacceptable to The Joan. She is much more mobile this morning so we decided we are not ready for the medical bed, and that is postponed. The Joan also feels well enough to go in the Toyota so the ambulance was cancelled. We are being prepared for discharge at the moment so should be on our way to 107 Main shortly.
    Hospice will be visiting this afternoon since they have to switch the morphine pump for theirs so we can send the current one back to Sloan. The oncology team believes that the extremely painful episode of the other evening could have been the cancer affecting nerves in her

abdomen, so we need to be prepared for that and oral drugs would not cut it.

The other good thing is that Ra went home to prepare the sunroom and cleaned it thoroughly. No doubt another ploy by The Joan to have that room sterilized—worked like a charm. I also understand that he has prepared the porch furniture for the warm weather as well—another unexpected bonus.

So before we check out, your Pearl today is again compliments of The Reading School of Nursing, circa 1950. Remember, there is a 3 ft. by 3 ft. pad on top of the sheet in the hospital bed so:

JOANIE'S PEARL
"If you tuck the pad under the mattress a little, it doesn't scrunch under the patient."

With Love...

CHAPTER 11

In the early 1980s, The Siddha Yoga Foundation purchased many acres of property in a town near my parent's house. They refurbished an old Borsht Belt hotel in disrepair and created acres of amazing gardens my mom really appreciated. A guru was over the whole thing and people came from far and wide to do yoga and meditation retreats. There was lots of chanting and people dressed like they were from India even if they were from Brooklyn. Think what you want about this particular group or movement or religion or whatever it actually is, but those people could cook!

When the Siddha opened, the public was welcome to eat in the restaurant. No doubt they wanted the community to love them for having hundreds of acres but without having to pay property taxes. A lot of my parents' friends wouldn't go to the ashram—they were afraid it was a cult and there would be Kool-Aid involved. But the Pizanos appreciated the inexpensive and very delicious vegetarian food too much, so we ate there often.

I was in middle and high school at the time and admittedly always watching my back and my cup of tea to make sure nobody slipped me a mickey. Everyone did seem very peaceful and friendly—oddly friendly, like too-good-to-be-true friendly. In any event, you can kind of identify those people if you see them on the "outside" like at the drugstore getting a pack of cigarettes (just kidding—they wouldn't do that in public) because of the way they dressed in Indian prints and loose fitting clothing. They also wore super comfortable yet unfashionable footwear as defined by Hollywood standards.

* * *

Sara Pizano, MA, DVM

Wednesday, April 11, 2012 9:12 PM
TJC #47

Hi Everyone,

The Joan, though a little on the drugged side, is doing well today—all things considered. Yesterday was a long day for her but the trip home was uneventful except for what I will refer to as "the plant incident" (more on that later, after I update you on her condition).

The hospice admissions nurse visited when we arrived home yesterday. We are no longer using the two other services—Advanced Care or Sullivan County Public Health—as all services now fall under hospice. The reason for this is that they are the only organization that will manage an at home morphine pump.

The good thing about hospice is that you design the care you need and want—it's a one-stop shop. We can request them every day or once a week. There is also a nurse on call 24-hours a day who is available by phone or if needed, can come over in the middle of the night, and they supply all needed equipment and medications. The Joan's oncologist prescribes the medications so that team must approve any changes.

Our nurse's name is Padma. When she walked in, The Joan immediately asked her if she was a part of the Siddha Yoga Ashram. As an innocent bystander, you may think that was an innocuous question, however The Joan had an ulterior motive. She wants Sergie to get top dollar for 107 Main after she leaves for Heaven and thinks the ashram would make for an excellent real estate deal. The wheeling and dealing never ends. The long and the short of it was that Padma _did_ belong to the Ashram but has since parted ways. No further details were given.

So for now, we will see Padma every Monday so she can change the needle for the mediport. There are also other bureaucratic details and annoyances that I won't bore you with, but rest assured, they will be rectified. Let's just say I had to give a dissertation and plead our case regarding the need for electrolytes in the intravenous fluids via speakerphone to the CEO of Hospice of Orange and Sullivan County. Our wish was granted on a "trial basis." Fine, I'll take it!

So thankfully, The Joan is pain-free but not a happy camper that she is "too dopey" (in her words) to be a productive member of society (my words). She changed into a fresh nightie this morning but stayed upstairs resting and reading for the day. We are asking her doctor if the

CRI (constant rate infusion) of morphine can be reduced so she can get back to her many projects and to-do lists promptly. She would still have the ability to pump more morphine when needed, but we are hoping the lower chronic dose would not zap her energy so much.

Even more important than her to-do lists is that she is not as active, so does have some edema (swelling) in her ankles and feet. Since she has minimal fat over her bones, we need to decrease the risk of bedsores as much as possible and being active is the best prevention.

The Joan got a major surprise yesterday as Annie (my childhood friend of thirty-plus years and currently a nurse practitioner) flew up from Florida to check on The Joan (Annie is another adopted daughter—I can't keep up!).

But your big news today is that The Joan felt hungry and drank a cup of Pero, had a muffin, some puree of chicken soup and a little protein shake!!! She clamped once for about 20 minutes and so far, so good. Continue to cross everything—I'm thrilled with this. Every calorie of glucose helps with her energy level.

So now for the "plant incident"... When Bobby-the-Doorman visited in the hospital, he brought The Joan a beautiful and unique plant (pictured below, or for some of you an attachment, and if you can see the picture, you can thank Roy). The Joan loves Bobby-the-Doorman _and_ flowering plants so this plant held sentimental and special value. One the way home, Sergie accidentally threw his jacket directly on the plant and snapped one flower stalk off! The Joan was mortified!

When we got home, Roy was pulling in from Miami via NJ and I told him about "the plant incident" and what a shame it was... yada yada. Roy then proceeds to tell me (you won't believe this one) that he did a science project in high school and grafted plants, so he could potentially fix the Bobby-the-Doorman plant! Please refer to previous The Joan Chronicles when I told you that Roy can fix anything and it is one of the many reasons that The Joan adores and is impressed with him. Not that I feel I have to prove to you that I am telling you the truth but in any event I am sending the picture 24-hour post graft as definitive proof that Roy can fix anything!!! (The graft is under the white tape in case you didn't know). Everyone needs a Roy. You may be able to borrow him if you live in the Hurleyville or Miami area—please call for availability.

Roy's ingenious plant graft

JOANIE'S PEARL
"Chinese chopsticks are the best utensil and easiest way to eat spaghetti or salad."

With Love...

* * *

In the 1970s, Joan and Serge joined the newly formed Sullivan Nuclear Opponents (SNO). You know the bumper sticker: "You can't hug kids with nuclear arms." That's where they met Rose.

Rose is a real connoisseur of luxury living. Roy is still baffled about the time Rose asked him if he could recommend a "good five dollar" (typed out so you would not think it was a typo) bottle of wine. Roy was speechless. Anyway, Rose alone provides endless entertainment without any effort. She is truly one of a kind.

* * *

Friday, April 13, 2012 6:35 PM
TJC #48

Dear Loved Ones,

The Joan is having what I call a "bad sandwich" day. The day started bad, then was good, and now is bad. That's a bad sandwich.

Yesterday she was able to eat a little yogurt for breakfast, a little gelato for dinner with a few snacks in between and a sip of Yuengling before bed. She clamped intermittently throughout the day (once for over an hour, which was great). Despite the fact that especially in the last few weeks her caloric intake has been so limited, I am happy to report her weight is remaining stable in the low 90s.

Yesterday, at The Joan's request and with her oncologist's permission, Padma (our hospice Nurse) cut the dose of morphine running continuously in half. It's really helped with The Joan's energy level and the dose she gets if she presses the button remains the same. I'm personally comfortable with this new setup, but The Joan is aiming for "zero" constant infusion of morphine. This leaves us with a vat of liquid morphine in the event that any of us need it and please don't share that with the authorities at the Drug Enforcement Agency.

The Joan was sick to her stomach this morning so had to take two different types of medications for the nausea. Since Joyce-the-Nurse was supposed to come up from the city to pick up the Japanese items, The Joan wanted to get up and get dressed, not to mention that Rose has entered the state and is back from California! All were supposed to convene at 107 Main for lunch.

At 6 AM, The Joan thought it would be best to get up, wash and dress in order to be ready to hostess her guests. I, on the other hand, thought it was best that vomit did not end up on the wall (or me—remember, I don't handle human stuff well) and managed to convince her that Joyce-the-Nurse and Rose would be completely understanding if she still had her nightie on and no eyebrows. They would even forgive her for hostessing from the king bed, under the electric blanket, if need be. So she rested some more and while cleaning up, Joyce-the-Nurse called to say she had a fever and sore throat so her road trip was postponed (don't worry—we already cashed the check—The Joan is a business woman, don't forget).

Thankfully, all the poltergeisted toxins in the stomach left early this AM so she was able to get washed and dressed and come downstairs by

10 AM and enjoy a light breakfast and some more gelato (yes, we are on a gelato kick, reliving our trips to Italia). Rose came for lunch and one of my previously tested recipes got rave reviews. Remember, most recipes have to be tested prior to Roy visiting because he has a very discerning (euphemism: picky) palette. I knew he would love the ginger-cilantro chicken meatballs in peanut sauce, so whipped up a batch with some basmati rice, ciabatta bread and salad. The Joan has to inspect all meals and/or new recipes, even though she can't eat them, and requested that I share the recipes with you.

So lunch was lovely and it is great to have Rose back on the east coast. Susan stopped by too and joined us for freshly baked macaroons. Unfortunately, for the last several hours, The Joan has been very painful and has been pressing the morphine pump frequently. She also had to take another dose of the nausea medication so we're hoping she has a comfortable night. We are certain, however, that this does not have anything to do with Rose being back on the East Coast.

JOANIE'S PEARL
"If you just smell food, like sweets, it can satisfy your craving without the calories."

With much love...

CHAPTER 12

It was the evening of May 23, 2011, and we knew my Nana would be passing on to Heaven very soon. Her three children kissed her good night before they left for the evening. Then the great-grandchildren and respective spouses lined up to say goodbye. One by one, they kissed her forehead, whispered their I love you's and choked back tears. It was an astonishing moment. How does one live ninety eight years and seven months (we called her "98.7") and be unconditionally loved by all their children, all their grandchildren and all their great-grandchildren, not to mention the whole town? Those moments were indescribable and the love palpable.

My Nana, Anne Marie Kiss, was born in Minersville, Pennsylvania, on August 23, 1913. When she was just five years old, her beloved mother, Mary Elizabeth Weber, died during the Great Flu Pandemic of 1918. Also called the Spanish Flu, this pandemic spread through Europe, Asia and the United States with unprecedented virulence. Nobody knows the actual number of deaths, but estimates range between fifty million and one hundred million people worldwide by the time the virus started to subside.

Sadly, my great-grandfather then married a woman who was not fond of my Nana and treated her poorly. For which reason, as my cousin Mark says, "How Nana grew to be the kindest/most gentle hearted/loving person she was, is well beyond me." A truer statement has never been uttered.

When she was eighteen, Anne Marie married my Pappy, Harold Hahn, of the "undertaker Hahns." They had three children: George the firstborn, followed by Mary Jane, and finally Joan.

Nana reading to her three young children

It was an innocent time in America and my Nana was truly one of the most innocent. I never heard her say a negative word about anyone or, for that matter, anything. If we were talking about something sad or difficult, she would say, "Enough of that sad talk, let's change the subject. Tell me something good." I remember telling her about a work situation when a colleague had treated me poorly. She said, "I can't understand why anyone would be mean to you. There's never a reason to not be nice. Ever." And that's how Nana lived.

My Nana was not judgmental and never got "cross," as she would say. She was the most loving person I knew. And that must have been true for everyone in Minersville, because the entire town loved her and called her Nana! But in 1971, when my Pappy was only sixty-two, my cousin Mark found him in the living room—he had suffered a massive heart attack and passed.

It was a shock to the family, and so unexpected. I don't think my Nana ever really recovered. Mark says we lost Pappy and a piece of Nana that day too. I believe that is a true statement. She never married again and devoted all her time to her children and grandchildren. Nana tried to live alone in the house she and Pappy shared, but it was just too lonely for her and she ended up moving in with my Aunt Jane, Uncle Joe and cousins Mark and Michelle in the funeral home.

In 2008, Nana was having trouble breathing and rushed to the hospital. She was in critical condition, or so we thought, and the priest was called at 3 AM to read her last rites. My aunts, uncles and cousins surrounded her bed, already starting to mourn their loss as they watched her blood pressure and heart rate drop steadily on the monitors. The priest left and all was quiet.

My Nana then reached up and took off her oxygen mask. Everyone leaned in to hear what they thought might be her final, profound words. She looked at my aunt and said, "You look nice tonight, Jane." There was a collective and quite massive sigh of relief. The next day the same priest walked by her room, fully expecting to see it empty, looked at my Nana and thought he saw a ghost! He was speechless. My Nana's vital signs soon improved enough to move out of the intensive care unit.

This was another time that God deliberately delivered me where I needed to be. I was already scheduled to arrive the same day, only a few hours after my Nana's last (but not really) rites were read. So I was able to be with her while she was in the hospital. What a blessing! My Nana continued to strengthen enough to be released from the hospital and went home with that priest shaking his head. Isn't it ironic when a "man of the cloth" is shocked by God's simple grace?

By the fall of 2010, my Nana had grown weaker and was again admitted to the hospital. Thankfully for me, God's grace kicked into high gear, as we already had our tickets to fly north from Florida to Pennsylvania for the Thanksgiving holiday. I was delivered to the hospital the very next day! I was very grateful to be able to care for my Nana while she was in the hospital and the nurses were grateful for Team Nana, as we called ourselves. They wanted to hire us to help them care for other patients. It broke my heart that there were other patients without a Team.

After the hospital, Nana went to rehab, but we were never able to get her strength back to where it needed to be. We had to make the very difficult decision of moving her to an assisted living facility. I'm sure this is a difficult decision for every family, but if I could have quit my job in Florida and cared for my Nana fulltime at home, I would have done it. So Nana moved into Luther Ridge, a beautiful assisted living facility just outside of Minersville.

Now this situation does require a little explaining: Since my Nana was no ordinary person, she would not receive ordinary care. My cousin Michelle, arrived in the morning around 9 AM, while Nana was having her breakfast. Michelle stayed with her for the morning and they ate lunch in the cafeteria (which looked more like a regular restaurant, if you ask me). After lunch, my Nana was ready for her siesta and Michelle would tuck her in.

Around 5 PM, my cousin Mark and his wife, Gaye, would arrive and take Nana to dinner in the cafeteria. After dinner, Mark got Nana settled into bed, adjusted her pillows until they were perfect, kissed her good night and turned out the lights. The Luther Ridge staff was amazed. They said they had never seen such a devoted family. My Nan was never alone when she was awake at Luther Ridge!

But as time marched on, my Nan grew weaker and was admitted to the hospital for the last time in May of 2011. And God did it again. He delivered me the day after she was admitted to the hospital—I had purchased the tickets several weeks before and was planning on taking Nana home for a break from Luther Ridge. But this time, Nana continued to fail rapidly. She had at least one stroke in front of me and started slurring her words and reaching for things that we couldn't see. Team Nana sat vigil by her side all day and the doctors began talking to us about keeping her comfortable instead of the goal of taking her home. But when her roommate told me she was up and calling our names in the middle of the night, I knew I couldn't leave her again.

Thankfully, Mark was able to get her moved into a private room so we could stay with her. For the next several nights, I slept next to her while Mark slept in a chair holding her hand. And it was during these days that I learned about the stages just before someone passes. First, when they are preparing to pass, they don't care if they are politically correct or not. Nana was telling it like it was for the first time in her life and it was a little shocking! You have to be prepared for this and don't take it personally—your loved one just needs to unload all that baggage! Please just continue to be loving during this stage.

Next, just before they pass, many people report seeing loved ones who have gone before them. While I was standing by my Nana's bed, she asked me who the gentleman standing next to me was. I told her nobody was there and she thought that answer was just fine. Later, though, I regretted saying that because I know now that it was a Spirit coming to get her. That was a lesson learned.

About 36 hours before my Nana passed, she got very agitated and jittery. For a full 24 hours, she couldn't stop moving and talking, and we wanted her to be able to rest and not be anxious, so the doctors prescribed intravenous morphine and Ativan. It helped her relax tremendously and she finally fell asleep. The doctors explained that an energy surge is very common when the end of your life on earth is near.

It was so important for me to be with my Nana when she passed. I wanted to be with her and hold her hand because I knew she was afraid to die. She never said as much but that's how I knew. Team Nana understood we were nearing the end.

My parents, aunt and uncle, then Nana's great-grandchildren left but the rest of us didn't feel we could. Four of my Nana's five grandchildren and three significant others surrounded her little hospital bed. We sat with her, hugged her limp body, held her hands, kissed her cheeks, touched her feet and told her it was OK to leave, even though we couldn't bear the thought. We told her that we would miss her and that we loved her but we would be OK. We watched her face lose color. We watched her blood vessels collapse. And just like that, my Nana stopped breathing. I couldn't imagine a more peaceful passing. I couldn't imagine being surrounded by more love. Team Nana rocked.

Little did I know then, that those amazing and blessed lessons were preparing me for when it was my mom's time. I will never forget them and am deeply grateful for that divine preparation as I held my mom's hand on her way to Heaven just fourteen months later.

Nana with her grandchildren, left to right, Rafael, Michelle,
Karen, me and Mark on her 90th birthday

CHAPTER 13

Saturday, April 14, 2012 8:54 PM
TJC #49

Hi Everyone,

My immediate disclaimer is that Roy and Sergie did some errands and brought back a Food TV network-approved bottle of Pinot Grigio (13% alcohol). Admittedly, I had a glass (OK, maybe a glass-and-a-half) which for anyone else (OK, maybe two glasses) would surely be a bottle (or more). I am a very cheap date and thus cannot be held responsible for the content of tonight's chronicles.

First, foremost and sadly, The Joan is not having a good day. Let me begin with a recap: During the hospital stay she experienced a super-horrible painful episode that lasted hours and was very difficult to manage. I was not leaving Sloan (and would have risked arrest) without some sort of IV intervention—legal or illegal. We left with the morphine pump (legally obtained for all you worrisome attorneys on the list), as you know, but The Joan was very unhappy with her level of "dopiness," in addition to which she went a couple of days without severe pain so didn't think she needed the CRI. Her oncologist approved cutting the CRI in half, but if needed she could still press that little button every 10 minutes for another smack of IV morphine. Fine. So the dose was cut in half yesterday morning.

This morning she just felt "lazy" and said she would stay in bed for her first IV bag of fluids, then come downstairs for the second. Unfortunately, beginning early afternoon, she was very painful so has pressed the pump many times since.

If you have never spent time with a loved one taking IV morphine, legal or illegal, I will tell you how it goes (come to think of it, I never did experience the illegal part of a loved one shooting up so can only comment on the legal experience). Initially they will tell you, it's not working. Then they will talk a lot—Team Nana hears what I'm saying. They talk about things that happened years ago that you yourself (with only the 13% alcohol Pinot Grigio in your system) forgot that you even remembered. The Joan is also focused on de-cluttering, sale prices on her Craig's List items, the future yard sale and giving loved ones her most beloved items before she leaves for Heaven. Directions are given without ceasing, so many conversations are of the instructional nature.

But here's the kicker and subsequently, the problem. Now The Joan is saying that she shouldn't have said to cut the CRI in half. She is suffering from "regret-itis." Whatever decision she makes, she later regrets. But the problem, my dear loved ones, is that there is no right answer and there is no wrong answer. Cancer is impossible.

So today The Joan consulted Annie, the other adopted daughter and Nurse Practitioner. The Joan was seeking medical advice: How long should she wait while taking morphine to have some beer? Being a good friend to Annie, I interceded and said: A) she was on CRI morphine so it wasn't a matter of when she pumped, B) we sort-of-kind-of got the blessing from our medical team who said "beer-schmeer, just keep the clamp open," and C) I was certain that question did not appear on her Nurse Practitioner test so it wasn't possible for her to answer! So The Joan chugged-a-lugged, just a few ounces, to quench her thirst. Remember, it's five o'clock somewhere. Anywho, The Joan pumped enough that she is now, thankfully, passed out cold.

JOANIE'S PEARL

"If your stairs are carpeted, vacuuming is simply not enough to keep them clean. Wipe each stair with a wet rag to get the accumulated dust in the crack too."

Much, much love...

* * *

Tuesday, April 17, 2012 10:32 PM
TJC #50

Hello Dear Loved Ones,

Lots to report, so I'll start with the good news. The Joan went on a field trip today! Short, but a field trip it was. The Joan needed to go to the bank and meet with a bank officer, then Sergie and I took her to the new and improved Monticello Dunkin' Donuts—a brand new building! Sergie, as you can imagine, is a longtime devoted patron (and no doubt helped to fund that new building) and confessed that he regularly gets a latte and chocolate covered donut while running errands. The Joan, on the other hand, has never stuck so much as her big toe in the DD building, old or new. She declined any Boston Creams as that craving appears to have passed.

Serge and Joan at Dunkin' Donuts

Yesterday, The Joan didn't pump any morphine but did hit the sauce before bed. The fizzless Yuengling, she says, helps to "settle" her stomach—okie dokie—whatever it takes. Today was a three-pump day, which isn't bad and I think we are all OK with the half-dose of the constant rate infusion (CRI) as The Joan is much more coherent and functional. On the first CRI dose, I found her with one dark blue and one light blue slipper. GASP! Need I say more? That's serious.

So overall, The Joan is doing better than I expected, but unfortunately not getting the calories in her as she was pre-hospital visit. As of two days ago she was 88 pounds. She is quite ambulatory, goes down the stairs (in the AM) and up the stairs (in the PM) and is still able to care for herself, which is a blessing in itself.

Now folks, it's time for your first Patient Advocate Lesson. At some point in your lives, you will be caring for a loved one, or need care yourself, and it's very important that the Patient Advocate (PA) is well informed. I tell you this because it can make a huge difference for your advocatee (not sure if that's a word, but it's mine now).

When a person isn't eating or drinking well, they feel weak and tired because they are dehydrated, for sure, but also missing out on important electrolytes like potassium and magnesium. Also, remember, the brain can't live without glucose (sugar). The longer your advocatee remains strong and active the better, because a whole host of secondary problems may otherwise manifest, such as bed sores that can become infected, pneumonia, etc.

In addition, the advocatee will feel lousy without those electrolytes and glucose. Being dehydrated and feeling weak also limits their ability to make good decisions about their care, so you have to have extra patience and remember that. Even though they are "the patient," they need your patient guidance, though they may not always realize it.

When The Joan is hospitalized, her fluid bags have all three of those (potassium, magnesium and glucose). When hospice took over the day we got home, I was surprised to see the fluids they delivered had no electrolytes and no glucose. Then I found out there were two prescriptions. The one dated first ordered electrolytes and glucose, but a more recent prescription was just for plain saline. By law, the most recent prescription overrides any previous ones. Mmmm?

So I started asking questions and called the doctor's office. They said, "We prescribed the glucose and electrolytes but hospice did not approve them." Hospice then told us they are considered "medications." So once I found an able-bodied volunteer to hold me back, I ended up giving a very nice and very calm dissertation to our local Sullivan/Orange County Hospice CEO and staff on speaker phone defending the first prescription.

Our hospice nurse was very supportive and a great advocate. I explained that these were not medications and certainly not treatment for the cancer but just basic electrolytes and glucose to help her feel better and it was my understanding that such a fabulous/amazing/perfect/ respected organization such as Sullivan/Orange County Hospice would really want their patients to feel as good as possible. The Joan had told me to "lay it on thick."

So, finally, after a closed door meeting, they agreed to a "trial" and wanted to make sure we understood they were really stretching here. After showering them with praise and thanks (through clenched teeth admittedly), a call back to the doctor's office converted the first prescription into a new prescription. Now, mind you, this is still a work in progress because the IV fluids were delivered with the electrolytes but without the glucose, so I have to go through steps two and three again but... my point?

I am not telling you this to float my boat or so you think I'm fabulous, but so you can question and clarify what you or your loved one needs. The Joan was diagnosed (and late at that) only because she kept insisting something was wrong even though several doctors said she was fine. We now are responsible to micro- and macro-manage our health care and you should learn and benefit from what we learn.

OK, I'm down from my soap box and leaving you with a Joanie Pearl reminded to me by our dear friend Audrey who was our neighbor from 1965 through 1971 on Union Street in Fair Haven, Vermont. Audrey says that The Joan taught her this Pearl way back then and Audrey has utilized it ever since:

JOANIE'S PEARL
"Always mow your grass in a circle so you mulch as you cut. When you're done, there is no need to rake."

With Much Love...

* * *

Thursday, April 19, 2012 8:03 PM
TJC #52

Attention The Joan Chronicles monitors: I apologize sincerely that TJC were mis-numbered. There were two #50s and no #51. If only that were the worst thing that could happen today!

So, all you Joanie Fans, this is actually number 52 and I would be delighted if nobody noticed. Where to begin?

Yesterday, The Joan's brother, George, sister-in-law, Teddy, sister, Jane and niece, Michelle, visited. As an added bonus, Michelle brought lunch and we carbo loaded on Palermo's special garlic rolls, eight boxes of pasta, chicken Marsala and salad! You can probably smell our garlic breath from 107 Main—it was fabulous! Michelle also treated The Joan to the last two pieces of Peanut Butter Cream Pie... to die for... still labeled "Joanie ONLY." That should supply her necessary calories and glucose for the next two weeks (OK, admittedly, I tasted it only to make sure it was an appropriate admission to the menu and I can attest that it was delish).

Yesterday was a good sandwich day: Good AM, not good in the afternoon and good evening (a perfect sandwich day would be good/good/good). Anyway, The Joan seems to be losing energy and getting painful mid-afternoon around 2 PM. So, after the carbo-loading and family visit yesterday, The Joan laid down to "rest" for several hours. I can confirm deep breathing and REM but The Joan will not likely admit to that. I understand but am only communicating this so you know the good news. The Joan was not feeling well and was painful and pumping (morphine) before the snooze then... voila!... she was renewed when she woke up late afternoon. PTL! (that's "Praise The Lord" for future reference).

Today she was downstairs, dressed and ready to greet the day at 8 AM. We entertained Rose, Susan and... the cable guy. Yes, people, I have been holding out on the big announcement until everything was in place but it now seems fitting. In addition to the push-button phone, the digital frame and streaming Netflix (thank you, Roy!), we now have... double drumroll... DVR capabilities (sort of)!!!!! OK—I'm working on some technical difficulties but Lord knows when I watch TV... all 45 minutes of it per week... I refuse to watch commercials and needed the capability to fast forward through them.

So I presented my case to Joan and Serge and explained how it would enhance their lives and save them valuable time... yada, yada. So now, we DVR and FF and it's fabulous! Can you get a load of the new and high-tech 107 Main? Pretty soon it will be a Smart House and we will be able to start the laundry while shopping at Walmart.

So The Joan's cravings this evening included a very baked potato with sour cream (and I mean a lot) and butter (and I mean a lot) with several *four ounces of the Yuengling. It seems the four ounces are going down quite smoothly and more frequently than previously assumed, as we are now about to down the last bottle in the case. No matter, there's more where that came from. And let me tell you, it's never the wrong time for Peanut Butter Cream Pie, so dinner included a couple of servings.*

JOANIE'S PEARL

"It's best to eat a huge and nutritious lunch at noontime then have a small snack at dinnertime. You will lose weight, and in addition will not feel stuffed when you go to bed."

Much Love...

* * *

Saturday, April 21, 2012 4:56 PM
TJC # 53

Hello Joanie Fans,

Two nights ago, The Joan couldn't sleep and was up from 1 AM. Yesterday, she fell into a deep sleep before 4 PM and pretty much slept until this morning. That was despite the addition of glucose into the IV fluids yesterday (PTL!), but even that extra kick of sugar couldn't keep her awake in the face of sheer exhaustion. Even getting dressed and showered is very tiring now.

She did wake up long enough last night to have a little dinner, compliments of Susan. Susan brought us beef stew with all the "Joanie-approved" vegetables (we'll overlook the few kernels of corn and one mushroom) so into the blender it went with some water to ease it into a puree. The Joan, although groggy at the time, really appreciated the new menu item and the protein is really good for her as she is eating fewer overall calories these days.

Also yesterday, The Joan's Physician's Assistant, Linda Thompson, stopped by since we were worried that The Joan was taken off her blood pressure medication. Linda was so sweet to come over and thankfully, left her 100-plus pound American Bulldog in the car. I was even more thankful that little peanut was in the car after Linda told us that as a puppy he was playing fetch with his dog sitter, playfully ran into her returning the stick, and ripped a tendon in the poor lady's knee that required surgery! I had to put my foot down. There will be no jumping on The Joan.

Linda and The Joan had a nice visit, discussed the blood pressure issue for about two minutes then the merits of The Mutual of Omaha's Wild Kingdom in the back of 107 Main for the next thirty. They mourned Earl-the-Squirrel—The Joan's first squirrel love who would come for his peanuts when called and was always very polite, unlike the other neighborhood squirrels. Unfortunately, poor Earl met his maker during an incident with a Chevrolet, and The Joan says she hasn't met a squirrel like Earl since...a reminder to savor those special friendships. Anyway, oh yes, the blood pressure... Linda doesn't think The Joan needs the meds so I'm checking it daily and today it was normal again. Yay!.

Unfortunately, The Joan woke up sick to her stomach this morning but recovered fairly quickly and ate a little breakfast later on. She was able to come downstairs in her jammies and has been in a deep sleep for several hours now. I'm not sure what to make of this Rip Van Winkle type behavior and was hoping the glucose in the fluids was going to give her a little energy boost. The Joan continues to be annoyed with herself for "not getting enough done," while I argue she is accomplishing a great deal. When you speak to her next, please pick her up in Regretsville and drop her off at 107 Main.

The weather has been just beautiful and raise your hand if you appreciate the warm sun as much as I do! Just as I suspected, The Joan was the only one to not raise her hand—she's a polar bear. (OK, admittedly she's sleeping but I'm telling you as fact, she prefers the dead of winter!)

The Joan and I have also started inspecting the state of the estate and discussing what should be planted where. Although I love to garden, I've never really had anything more than potted plants so I still need coaching to discern weeds from perennials or annuals or whatever they're called. Don't want to ruin next year's crop and I'm big on pulling out everything so it looks neat—very dangerous habit. We'll be planting herbs to cook with (and cheating by planting ones that are already big so don't be too impressed) and lots of flowers, so hopefully The Joan will like the end result. Today's Pearl is in honor of The Joan's love of gardening:

JOANIE'S PEARL
"Human urine poured in your garden will deter the deer and prevent them from nibbling on your precious plants!"

Much Love...

* * *

Monday, April 23, 2012 8:13 PM
TJC #54

Hello Dear Loved Ones,

We're still here and hanging on but The Joan is eating far less than she was. Because her caloric intake is so low, she doesn't have a lot of energy these days. Today she woke up tired, but dressed and came downstairs before 8 AM, then napped on the couch and missed most of the exciting Today program (no worries—it's DVR'd!). This afternoon she "rested" and, rest assured, heard every word we muttered even though we thought she was "sleeping." This could have been a simple question regarding garbage can lids but The Joan piped in, "Just buy the lid, don't have to replace the whole can", or "It's in the top drawer on the right", if someone was looking for something. The Joan doesn't like to miss anything.

Yesterday was a five-hour nap day. That was solid REM sleep but when The Joan awoke, she announced that she was ready to have some fun. In The Joan's world, this means a rousing game of Rummikub. Unfortunately in Ra and Sergie's world, it simply does not—no other way to say it. I tricked them into coming downstairs, saying something about how The Joan needed help, but it wasn't a total lie—she needed them to help her play Rummikub! It was so exciting that I started falling asleep in the middle of the game around my designated bedtime (9:30). We are partying hearty here at 107 Main—it's crazy day and night.

Besides the "laziness", The Joan has been struggling with being nauseous a lot so that hasn't helped the ol' appetite. Tonight her craving was mashed potatoes so basically anything in the kitchen with calories was added. She's had a hard time keeping her eyes open so went upstairs to "read" in bed before 7 (Read is in quotations because it basically means she props herself up in bed with an open book and the lights on but sleeps anyway... when you try to turn the lights off, she says she doesn't want to go to bed so early and you have to gently point out the obvious—that she already <u>was</u> sleeping so it's a moot point.) Anywho, although she was barely awake post carbo-loading with the mashed potatoes, I asked her if she wanted anything else to eat. Hardly able to speak and mind you, with her eyes closed, she said, "Yes...my book, my phone and some beer." Well, I didn't see that one coming and had to make a mental note to take a pad and pen the next time I asked—it's hard to keep up.

Important Sidebar: The Joan is almost up to date on The Joan Chronicles and has only one complaint (phew). She feels that I have unfairly painted her as a lush and debates that she really doesn't drink that much beer. I assured her that none of you think she has a drinking problem and furthermore nobody will be contacting the authorities RE: controlled drug and alcohol use, and that it was all in good fun (although I was serious about the increase from four to six ounces).

JOANIE'S PEARL
"When storing fancy beaded purses, place them in plastic Ziplock bags to protect the beading."

Much, much love...

* * *

Wednesday, April 25, 2012 10:34 PM
TJC #55

The Joan has not been well yesterday and today, sick to her stomach and not able to really get any calories in. More tomorrow and will include two pearls.

Much love...

* * *

Thursday, April 26, 2012 7:43 PM
TJC #56

To The Joan's Collection,

We have had a very rough couple of days but The Joan is back! She was very ill this morning and took both Compazine for vomiting and morphine for the pain. She slept most of the day, in and out. When she woke up this evening she was ready for her chicken soup puree followed by the Haagen Dazs/applesauce/real whipped cream dessert! Since she has not had anything to eat in several days, she felt it wise not to push her luck and did not clamp.

The Joan wasn't able to get out of bed today except for a few trips to the lavatory. We changed her nightie and Sergie put a layer of Eucerin cream over her thin bones. That stuff is like Crisco in the big can and in fact I am told that in the olden days, Crisco was used to prevent bed sores—I can also report that Crisco is cheaper than the Eucerin in case you are ever in a bind. The Joan's only concern was that she might slip out of the bed like a greased pig (OK, I added the pig part but she did say the rest).

Now, kids, it's time for your Patient Advocate Lesson Number 2. Remember that I told you that Sloan would not prescribe the intravenous drugs to prevent the vomiting that worked in the hospital? I thought it was against the law but in fact it was a Sloan policy. (Sidebar question: How many people really want to shoot up at home with the exception of addicts? I think most people would rather be hospitalized especially since most don't have their own live-in veterinarian like The Joan does.)

At all costs, I wanted to prevent another hospital stay for The Joan over something as silly as a few milliliters of an injectable drug a day. So I called The Joan's Nurse Practitioner and local health care provider, connected her with hospice and voila! the intravenous Zofran to stop the vomiting was delivered to our door by noon. My point and Lesson Number 2: Don't stop asking questions on behalf of your loved ones!

Also, use phrases like "Can you please explain how this process works?" and "Is there any other way this can happen?" and "What an amazing organization you have". And PS, be reeeeallly nice. I haven't sobbed on the phone yet but will resort to it if need be. The Joan has coached me to "lay it on thick" and use her cancer to our advantage shamelessly, as it has to provide something positive!

So tonight The Joan feels better than this morning but feels that she doesn't have much time left. So... serious issues had to be discussed and she asked me what I decided about the desserts for the "after party" luncheon for you all, following The Event. I told her (truthfully) that I had not thought about it, but that Anne's in Minersville makes great pies and I have a thing for pies. She agreed that yes, Anne makes great pies so there should be a Peanut Butter Cream Pie and an Apple Pie along with the Cheesecake. Remember, it was imperative that there be <u>three</u> desserts and I am to make sure there is enough!

JOANIE'S PEARL
"You should have one dish towel used only to dry the dishes and one dish towel used only to dry your hands and NEVER mix them up."

With Love and Prayers...

CHAPTER 14

Before I moved back to 107 Main to care for my mom, her virtual communication consisted of Sergie printing out an email from a friend and my mom snail-mailing a response. Her only potential interest in the computer was learning how to sell things on eBay. The first time we tried to teach her how to use a mouse, she dragged it across the table and practically up the wall! Remember, people... nothing is obvious to the uninformed.

During these months, with friends and family receiving TJC, pictures and emails were flying all over the place. Loved ones sent videos of new babies or special events, lots of pictures or just an email to say they were thinking of The Joan. Sometimes she was too tired to look at an email so I ended up printing them and inserting them in her master copy of TJC in chronological order, of course, so she would "get" all the jokes. She loved it and read it like a book.

This three-ring binder would ultimately end up being over 400 pages and The Joan kept it next to her and constantly showed different entries to friends and family when they visited. Not only did it make her feel connected, but she was literally amazed at how much everyone cared about her. She said she had no idea how truly loved she was until she was sick with the cancer. I was shocked to learn that—I always knew it!

That book provided an endless stream of positive energy and love. I've noticed while bearing witness to several loved ones about to cross over, that they are only interested in the positive. They want to look at beautiful things, think about positive things and live in a happy state. My mom loved Christmas and gardening so would always have a magazine next to the bed that she could look through. It didn't matter if the magazines were ten years old, it was the pictures and stories that were timeless to her. Keep it in mind if you are helping a loved one deal with this inevitable time in their life. You can always get magazines or books at thrift stores for pennies or ask friends and family to lend you some.

* * *

Thursday, April 26, 2012 8:16 PM
TJC #56 Addendum

Thank you to my good friend Donna Butler, who politely reminded me that I promised two pearls but only delivered one this evening so here is your addendum Pearl:

JOANIE'S PEARL
"When your daughter is going on a date make sure you tell her not to shave her legs."

* * *

Friday, April 27, 2012 8:50 PM
TJC #57

Dear Loved Ones,
Today The Joan felt pretty good. The day started early at 6 AM with a bout of nausea that was quickly diminished with the new and improved intravenous Zofran... yay! After we all snoozed a couple more hours, The Joan ventured downstairs. Mobilizing The Joan is a family affair now as there are many moving parts, tubes and expensive electronics that must follow her closely and not get stepped on or forgotten. Mobilizing down the stairs takes at least two family members. I typically stay in the back so Ra or Serge end up on the down side (hey—you never know when The Joan might slip and fall and they simply have more meat on them—it's a simple safety precaution).
Then one of us will be the IV pole and that person always has to stay north of The Joan on the stairs so the bag is higher than her

catheter—it's all about the gravity. Finally, she carries the gastric bag with the fashionable cover like a purse over her wrist and one member of the entourage will wear the $4,000 morphine pump (north or south since it's battery operated and not gravity dependent). Again, in case The Joan accidentally squashes a family member, one of you loved ones may be asked to step in, so it's essential that you are prepared both physically and mentally.

Overall, The Joan felt pretty good in the "new normal" realm of existence. Characteristic of The Joan she has analyzed this in detail and has concluded that it's because (1) she rested in bed all day yesterday and slept most of it, (2) even though her clamp has remained open, eating food and drinking has given her a little more energy, and (3) not being nauseous is a good thing (that's a bonus Pearl). So today was a downstairs-nightie-day and The Joan is considering alternating her schedule between up and down since she feels she needs to recuperate from all the excitement downstairs.

But dear ones, the very sad news for today is that The Joan doesn't feel she'll be able to clamp the G-tube again since she feels that her obstructions are worsening. Still, she is enjoying eating even though very little of it will get through now. I think it's good to do the act of eating and feel stuff in your stomach—just the physical presence of food in the stomach helps her to feel a little full even if it's temporary. On the good side, we were able to get a second drug for the nausea intravenously (Ativan) that The Joan was taking orally but couldn't often take if she was super nauseous. I also want you to know that The Joan is so grateful (and still somewhat in awe) that both Ra and I have been here these last few months. Roy will be coming next week and she's excited for him to work on some plumbing issues she is confident he can accomplish even though he is an engineer... and oh yes, she adores him too.

JOANIE'S PEARL

"Shampoo is extremely concentrated so feel free to dilute it even to one part shampoo, nine parts water. It will still wash your hair perfectly and save you a bunch of money."

With Love...

* * *

Sara Pizano, MA, DVM

Saturday, April 28, 2012 10:24 PM
TJC #58

Hi Everyone,

    The Joan was very "lazy" today but still came downstairs (see TJC #57 for instructions). The nausea is worsening and today she agreed to all three of the medications. Thankfully, the trifecta kept her comfortable and she enjoyed a spa foot massage and soak in one of those fancy electronic foot massage buckets in the sun room. She is continuing to go through papers and came across one piece you will not believe.

    Recently, she received a note and a piece of paper from someone in Minersville, Pennsylvania, The Joan's hometown. This person was in the Minersville Public Library, opened a book and found this piece of lined notebook paper. On the top it said "Joan Hahn, Homework, November 5, 1945." WHAT?! Swear this is a true story and if Roy were here he would figure out a way to scan it to you. On the front was her homework assignment and on the back this poem:

    "Good Night Sweet Jesus, the One I love best.
    I have finished my work and now I must rest.
    You have blessed me today, now bless me tonight,
    And keep me from danger, until morning light.
    Good morning dear Jesus, this day is for you,
    So I ask you to bless all I think, say and do."

    Isn't this remarkable? I can't get over it. And we can glean so much information from this. First, the Minersville Public Library is in desperate need of new books—that book has been on that shelf for at least 67 years!!!! That alone is remarkable, not to mention it is proof that the library has never had a fire that destroyed all the books in at least 67 years and finally, The Joan must have had to do her homework again since she left this copy in the book and she couldn't print another copy from her Mac.

    I just can't wrap my little pea brain around the fact that the little piece of paper was folded in that book on that shelf in that library and that someone found it six decades later and knew how to find Joan Hahn. Actually, that last part is not so crazy since very few people leave or enter the tiny hamlet of Minersville. It's just one of those towns where everyone knows everyone and this is proof! I'm submitting this story to "Ripley's Believe it or Not" even though I still can't believe it!

JOANIE'S PEARL
  "When getting your blood pressure taken, don't cross your legs."

Much, much love...

* * *

Monday, April 30, 2012 7:35 PM
TJC #59

Hello Dear Ones,
  The Joan continues to have high peaks (walked in the driveway today) and low valleys (very weak with pain and nausea) all in the same day, so things continue to change hour to hour. Her voice isn't as strong as it was so it's getting harder for her to speak on the phone. If you do get to talk with her, just remember to do most of the talking and keep it short (I know, more instructions, but as House Manager I am in charge of the Standard Operating Procedures). The Joan loves to stay informed and know what's going on in your lives.
  Thank goodness that someone found the heat switch and it was around 60 degrees here today—still fleece weather but a little less than Uggs boots. The Joan was able to sit in the sun for a little while on the front porch whilst I weeded frantically before the next frost, probably tonight.
  Tomorrow, we'll prepare the front circle and hopefully cash in on that $80 credit from the gardening center The Joan secured. When The Joan gives the green light, we'll plant! Of course, with the last heat wave (when it reached 62), I was full steam ahead, ready to plant all kinds of flowers, in total denial the temperature might drop again. Then The Joan gently reminded me it was still winter here and too early. Gasp! More cold? I fear my blood may freeze.

JOANIE'S PEARL
"Drift wood is a nice addition to any garden. Besides the added texture and depth, it takes up space so you can save money on plants."

Much love...

* * *

It is really important to communicate all your loved ones' needs to the hospice staff. They may not always be able to accommodate a request, but often can make suggestions or referrals. I think my mom was in a unique and blessed position. My dad had retired years before and my brother and I were choosing to stay with her between jobs. My mom really appreciated that and felt immensely blessed by our presence and efforts to care for her.

When she became too weak to take a shower, she leaned her head over the kitchen sink so we could wash her hair. But soon, even that proved challenging. We didn't think to mention it to our hospice nurse, Padma, but when my mom said she wished she could wash her hair more often, Padma brought us a shampoo cap. This is an ingenious idea! It looks like a shower cap but when you put it on your head and massage it, it washes and rinses your hair clean! We wish we knew about it sooner.

* * *

Tuesday, May 1, 2012 11:31 PM
TJC #60

Dear Loved Ones,
Today The Joan got washed, dressed and even had a shampoo and condition. Her hair is quite wavy, which as you know is a big deal to her. She has always had poker straight hair and wished for curly. Eating the crust on bread never actually worked. (Did anyone ever try to bribe any of you straight-haired girls with that one?)
Now, dear ones, I'm sorry to have to say what I am about to say. The Joan feels she is now totally obstructed. It's been well over a week

since she clamped the G-tube so is getting minimal nutrition. Our hospice nurse, Padma, was here today to change the mediport needle for the IVs and The Joan was wondering why she has been losing her voice. Also, the other day, The Joan was awake but sort of in a dream state while speaking to us. Padma explained that it's really common for those things to happen when you are close to the end of your life. It's the natural progression of your body preparing for Heaven.

It pains me to tell you all these things and give you news you don't want to hear, but I feel compelled to tell you a story about my cat Lucas— sort of like, "Everything I Needed to Learn, I Learned from my Cat" (instead of kindergarten... although that was a great year!).

If you really do what I did, I promise it will help you. Lucas was a special cat. Not your run-of-the-mill-there's-a-regular-cat but one of those amazing creatures that you are sure knows "more." He was The Joan's favorite (don't tell Sebastian that) and he died a very tragic and unexpected death. I was overwhelmed with grief, just so devastated. You think over and over "how tragic, how sad, how horrible," and sometimes people are tempted to be mad at God for taking their loved one away prematurely or in an unfair way.

Then one day, like a light switch, I thought about how grateful I was that God had blessed me with such a special cat. I kept thanking Jesus for giving me such an amazing gift for the time He did. When I thought about Lucas after that it was from a place of deep appreciation and gratitude and it lifted my grief like a veil in the wind. It was never as painful to think about him after that and it's helped me through some other tough times too.

So that's my advice to you. Come from a place of gratitude. Many of you on this list have known The Joan her whole life. More of you have known her for many decades. Be grateful for that. Be grateful for the memories of so many amazing times, holidays, advice, laughs, meals, joy and sorrows shared. And for now, just be grateful that The Joan is still here and continuing to spit out Pearls for you all.

The Joan has few regrets and has loved the life she has lived with all of us. She feels immensely blessed and looks forward to Heaven. She is especially looking forward to meeting my Nana's birth mother who passed when Nana was only five years old. I expect that Nana and her BFF Florence will be playing Peanuckle and are waiting to welcome The Joan home with open arms. I'm sure my Uncle Joe will be smoking, but *that's OK because cigarettes are not bad for you in Heaven. The Joan is not afraid and that should help comfort you. She worries more about all of us on a variety of levels than herself (remember, for example, "If we put the hospital bed in the sun room, where will visitors sit?").*

God bless you for your friendship and love. The Joan is really grateful for all of you!

JOANIE'S PEARL

"When cutting up a credit card, dispose of the pieces in different garbage cans so no one can find them, put them back together and use them."

With much love and gratitude...

$$* * *$$

Wednesday, May 2, 2012 9:45 PM
TJC #61

Dearest Friends and Family,

The Joan had a really good day with no nausea and minimal pain. There was even an impromptu trip to the basement! This occurred during Susan's visit, but much to her dismay.

Backstory Sidebar: *When the sunroom was built, for a reason I cannot explain, the electrician thought only one plug was needed for a 500-square-foot multipurpose room. Any aberration from one lamp or anything over one amp plugged in will blow a fuse. Fine... so we adapt and during the cold weather from August 1 to June 30, there are multiple extension cords running on the floor of the sunroom like a rat's nest to power a variety of space heaters. Apparently I, not being properly informed, may have inadvertently plugged in a _____ (fill in the blank), and poof: no power.*

OK, back from the backstory: So Ra, being the explorer in the family, made the trek to the basement to flip the switch, after extensive training by The Joan on the flipping of this particular switch. He returned from his journey feeling triumphant but alas: no power. This trek was repeated multiple times yielding the same non-result.

The Joan fretted over this for days, convinced that the switch was not flipped properly. And, being The Joan, she was not about to pay $100 for an electrician to visit and flip that freakin' switch himself! I gave her option one: Roy would be arriving next week and he would flip the switch and tell her if a higher electrical authority was needed.

I cannot confirm that The Joan actually processed this option, but she decided that the more common sensical thing to do would be to flip the switch herself. Since others in the family, who shall remain nameless, did not approve of The Joan making the trek to the basement, I thought it wise to rope Susan in as a spotter while they were out of the room.

So, we started the descent with Susan to the south (I had to be the IV pole to the north) and yikes!! Sergie caught us and started yelling out all kinds of instructions about danger and what we should and should not depend on for support on the way down. It was quite the scene. Once we were down (safe landing—phew), I knew we had an extra IV pole down there but alas, nebbish that I am, I didn't think to tidy up the basement before The Joan's trek. I can only do so much, people!

There were lots of questions about what this is doing there, and what that is doing here... yada yada. And poor Susan, not accustomed to accompanying The Joan on a non-carpeted surface, found it a challenge to keep up (she also suggested a video camera for proper documentation and comedic relief). The Joan was not slow. At least with the Queen there's a lot of waving and stopping to chat so the entourage has a moment to catch up. The Joan is more like a humming bird so you have to always be on guard for a change in speed and direction. Long story longer—The Joan flipped the switch and... OK... she had to cough up that $100 for the electrician's visit anyway.

Other than that, it was a typical day at 107 Main. I baked cookies, Sergie read his Kindle, The Joan wrote her obituary and Ra was on the computer. Beep, beep... backing up... Yes, The Joan is trying to accomplish as much as possible so we don't have to deal with these things, and completed her own obituary today. I know, very Adams Family, but remember, I already gave you the opportunity to unsubscribe. I did my best to warn you.

And just a few shout-outs to close: Thanks Mimi for pointing out that I spelled **Pinochle** wrong in TJC #60, but I intentionally had no patience for the computer's red underline under **Peanuckle**.

Sara Pizano, MA, DVM

Thanks to Susan who educated us this past weekend—the 101st anniversary of Crisco—that not only was Crisco used to prevent bed sores, but women used it as a face cream when it first came out. It is truly the wonder lard.

So on we go and I'm hoping tomorrow The Joan can accompany us to the gardening center to cash in on our free tree credit!

JOANIE'S PEARL
"Gardenia flowers floating in a bowl of water make your house smell great."

Much, much love...

* * *

Friday, May 4, 2012 9:45 PM
TJC #62

Hello Dear Ones,
I have to think back to yesterday now to catch you up. The Joan is feeling weaker now and though she dressed and came downstairs yesterday, she had to begin her nap a little early (around 1:30 PM) and it lasted a little longer (until 7:30 PM). I braced myself for her to wake... I knew what was coming.

She woke up, yawned and asked what time it was. For a fleeting moment, I considered lying and saying something like "3 PM" but then I figured she would catch on an hour later when it got dark outside. Oh boy... here goes:
Me: "It's 7:30" (then cupping my ears).
The Joan: "PM?!?!?"
Me: "Yes, PM" (having still heard through my cupped ears).
The Joan: "But I have THINGS to do!"
Me: "OK," (wearily) "Let's get started."
I'm not sure what was going on today but it was accidentally party central. Rose called to determine whether or not it was a good visiting day. Aunt Zizi called to determine whether or not it was a good visiting day. Brenda called to determine whether or not it was a good visiting day. And here's my disclaimer: unless you are arriving in the next six minutes,

I have no idea if it's a good visiting day and cannot be held responsible if The Joan is snoring by the time you arrive.

It just so happened that Rose, Brenda, Zizi and then Susan visited, so being the good caretaker that I am, I put them to work. "The Joan needs sun, girls, so why don't you all visit on the front porch?", I asked politely. So The Joan was able to rest in her lounge chair, have valuable visiting time with the girls, and get some sun to boot, showing that she truly did deserve "The Multitasker of the Year Award."

Unfortunately for me, Brenda showed up in her "teacher clothes" and claimed she was unable to help me unload the 450 pounds of mulch I had stashed in the trunk of the Toyota (3 for $10 at the Home Depot—DO NOT go to Shoprite, it's 3 for $12, the scammers).

And then, Zizi slips and says it's her birthday and The Joan is <u>mortified</u> that her card was not posted yet! So, being the dear friends that we are, we stuck a candle in the mousse cake that Zizi brought for The Joan and sang Happy Birthday to her after dinner! Desperate times call for desperate measures.

Speaking of mousse, I have to share this latest recipe I found for The Joan. She is eating minimal calories, so I am still trying to pack as many as possible into each bite. So here's the recipe for Dark Chocolate Mousse that I found, and I thought would be good for her, and she liked:

Dark Chocolate Mousse
(But I would call it "Serious Chocolate Pudding" instead)

12.3 ounce package of silken tofu, drained (<u>this </u>is why I liked this recipe for The Joan but I also think it's good for kids who like chocolate as it's an easy way to sneak in protein—Merisa—and I pinky swear to all you tofu haters that you will never know it's in there!)

3 ounces bittersweet chocolate, finely chopped

¼ cup unsweetened cocoa powder

¼ cup water

1 tablespoon brandy (we didn't have any brandy in the house and I voted "no" on adding Yuengling, so The Joan said to add her favorite Christmastime liquor—Harvey's Bristol Cream)

½ cup sugar

Puree the tofu until smooth (this is a really important step because if you don't there are little unsightly white specs in the mousse). Put the chopped chocolate, cocoa powder, ¼ cup of water and brandy in a saucepan or heat-proof bowl fitted over a pot containing one inch of barely simmering water. Stir frequently until melted and smooth then remove from heat. Mix in the sugar a little at a time until smooth. Add the chocolate mixture with the tofu and puree until smooth. Cover and refrigerate at least an hour.

Disclaimer: The above recipe came out more like a super chocolate, chocolate pudding instead of mousse so if that's your thing, you can stop there. At 107 Main, we did a taste test so the above is called Recipe "A." Then I did the following:

Whip ½ pint of heavy cream until almost stiff (and way before it turns to butter) then add 1 tsp of sugar and ½ tsp of super great quality vanilla and whip until it peaks.

* * *

For those of you unfamiliar with this highly complicated recipe, that's how you make whipped cream from scratch (Xiomara). I then blended the whipped cream into Recipe "A" and it looked and tasted like mousse (Recipe "B"). Our nuclear family, Rose and Brenda were split down the middle. Half preferred Recipe A and half liked Recipe B so pick your chocolate poison. I am a disgrace to women everywhere as I don't like chocolate and prefer vanilla.

So, overall, The Joan had a good day, and while we hosted Aunt Zizi's birthday dinner (all planned ahead of time... wink, wink), The Joan had to lie down. She did find the strength to participate throughout dinner, however, and threw in her two or four cents when needed. Thankfully she was well rested by the time the birthday mousse cake, Recipe A and Recipe B was served.

JOANIE'S PEARL

"To clean under difficult to reach places, like stoves and refrigerators, wrap a wet rag around the end of a yardstick."

With much, much love...

* * *

Monday, May 7, 2012 11:48 AM
TJC #63

Hello Dear Ones,

Sorry that I have been derelict in my duties as your informant. When we last left you, The Joan had been partying heartily (although she did try to snooze during part of the festivities). That was Thursday, so Friday was a Rip van Winkle day to make up for it. On Friday morning The Joan got dressed and came downstairs but then proceeded to sleep on the couch essentially from noon-9 PM, then went to bed for the night at 9:30. The good thing is that at least you know during that sleep time she was not nauseous or painful or she wouldn't have been able to sleep so soundly. And, once again, The Joan was not pleased with herself and at 9 PM asked "What the hell is going on?!?! I'm sleeping my life away".

Sidebar: Just don't tell The Joan I told you she cussed as she would be mortified. And oh yes, she is also mortified that you might think she wrote the poem to Jesus on the back of her homework in 1945. The Joan wants to clarify that she can't remember if she wrote the poem, just copied it or if Sister wrote it but suspects the handwriting is a little different than hers so that might be the case. I can only confirm it was on the back of her homework dated November 5, 1945. Phew—what a huge weight lifted!

We've been busy in the yard and Ra attempted to cut the grass for the first time. (Yay! I'm hoping that is an indication it will not snow again.) Unfortunately, the newly "fixed" tractor blew the belt that was just changed two days before and is now lawn art until the boys hoist it back on the truck for repeat repairs. I created a "grill circle" in the place where the famous above-ground pool previously resided (Does anyone want to *buy a pool? If so, please see Craig's List for our advertisement.) The Joan found my grill circle very impressive. Like I told you: mulch = magic.*

Today, I will be working on the front circle. The Joan is <u>giving away</u> hostas along with ground cover, so please stop by with a shovel and load some in your car—preferably today. I am not certain how all that can transpire, but I may include free lemonade while people are digging or may resort to paying people to take one. We also may be on the brink of cashing in on that free tree credit, so stay tuned for that excitement!

The Grill Circle

The Joan has been up since 4 AM today and is blaming my Chocolate Mousse consumed too late in the day yesterday for that. She's slightly exhausted so after lounging in bed this morning, made it downstairs to the sunroom to have her breakfast. Since we are somewhat off our peak/valley/peak/valley schedule day-to-day, I cannot predict what today, or for that matter, tomorrow may bring but one thing is for sure... thanks to *The Joan's over-the-top-extreme OCD (which I also inherited from her—fortunately or unfortunately depending on who you ask), the Pearls are never ending:*

JOANIE'S PEARL
"Wash your sweaters inside out to prevent them from pilling, and to keep them looking like new longer."

With much Love...

* * *

Wednesday, May 9, 2012 8:26 PM
TJC #64

Hi Everybody,
   The Joan's day began early at 5:30 AM with some discomfort. Fortunately, she was able to fall back to sleep and fortunately I was able to start weeding early, since I was unable to fall back to sleep myself.
   Sidebar question: *What do gardeners and golfers (at least this one) have in common? (See answer below, although I'm not certain I can actually classify myself as a gardener. I think I'm more in the bulldozer category and would label myself more of an exuberant and overenthusiastic weeder. There is a small, yet very good chance that I yanked out some Hollyhocks before finding out they have bloomed each year since before we moved to 107 Main in 1971. PS: If anyone has any mature Hollyhocks, I will gladly trade you for the hostas.)*
   Anywho, after an additional snooze, The Joan came downstairs but stayed in her jammies taking intermittent "rests" and snoozes throughout the day. Roy arrived today and will start his Joanie-Honey-Do-List tomorrow as he announced that today was a day of rest, even though it's not Sunday. The Joan is fine with that as she knows how productive and dependable Roy is and she is very excited about having closet doors again in the master bedroom.

JOANIE'S PEARL
"When cutting your grass, always start in the front of the yard in case the tractor breaks down (again). Then at least your

front yard will be mowed and the unsightly un-mowed parts will be behind the house and out of public view."

Sidebar answer: *The blister occurs in the same place on the thumb.*

Much Love...

The Hollyhocks in full bloom (old picture)

* * *

I am not exactly sure when you can qualify yourself as a "golfer." People often ask me if I am a golfer and I never know how to answer.

"Well, I golf", I might respond.... Does your handicap have to be a certain number to call yourself a "golfer?" All I know for sure about golf is that if it doesn't hurt when you hit the ball, then it's a good shot. At least for me, that is.

My parents always loved to hear about my golfing adventures. Like the time I "chipped in." I seriously "chipped in" from forty yards right into the clown's mouth! That was a highlight, as was the plaque I got another time in a tournament for "Closest to the Pin" in the Women's Category. Nobody has to know I had to use a seven iron to get on the green since I was about 150 yards away but regardless, I was "Closest to the Pin" out of all five women in the tournament with eighty men!

If I had to think of a low point, it would probably be on the driving range with my then-boyfriend, David (who could actually call himself a golfer, no question). He was grooming me to be a kick-ass player and wanted me to try his new $400 Ping driver. I stepped up to the tee, set the ball on the little plastic thingy and my swing was perfect (I know that because it didn't hurt) and the ball went perfectly straight over 100 yards. It was a thing of beauty.

The only problem was that the head of that new $400 Ping driver left in tandem with the ball. I was left holding only a straight stick, the remains of said driver. For a fleeting moment I did impress myself with how straight both the ball and the head of the driver traveled, and together no less. The shocked gaggle of men watching me turned their attention to my then-boyfriend, whose eyes were like saucers. I have to say that he was a big sport about it and I was off the hook because Ping fixes a broken driver for free!

My mom did not, however, appreciate the golf advice I gave our neighbor girls. In golf, you step away from the ball before you hit it and take a few practice swings to loosen your muscles. There are times, albeit few, that you might just air ball—that is, you miss the ball completely. In that case, I advised them to step back and stretch nonchalantly and pretend it was a practice swing! The Joan told them to ignore that piece of valuable advice.

CHAPTER 15

As my mom's caretaker, I found one of the most difficult things to achieve was the balance between rest and visitors. She never wanted to deny anyone a visit, but many days she just did not have the energy, or even worse, was feeling painful or nauseous. We never knew how her day was going to turn out, so predicting and making plans was nearly impossible. We just did the best we could and everyone understood that there was a possibility of last minute cancellations or abridged visits.

* * *

Thursday, May 10, 2012 8:10 PM
TJC #65

Hello Dear Loved Ones,
This morning The Joan was up and at 'em early, dressed and downstairs ready to greet the day. She had a nice in-home massage (how could that be bad?) followed by several loved ones visiting. The Joan is definitely improving in her ability to let company know she needs a nap. Sometimes she says things like "I have to lay down", and sometimes it happens more naturally and she has a narcoleptic episode. Either way, I always start the conversation if I see her eyelids closing, with "You know, Ma, so and so will understand if you have to take a snooze.....".
Nausea and pain continue to be intermittent and intense at times, but I am happy to report that her blood pressure has remained normal off her meds. We have a little electronic blood pressure kit—very cool—in a little

carrying case so I check The Joan's blood pressure every couple of days to make sure. Imagine my surprise when I opened the kit today in front of "other" family members and found one of my homemade chocolate chip cookies! I forgot I hid the last cookie from "other" family members (hint: not from me and not from Joanie). Dagnabbit, another hiding place exposed!

I also wanted to thank everyone for their feedback regarding the Pearls and how those gems are changing your lives. Donna Butler was out shopping for baby wipes (even though her children are in college) to clean the baseboards and thinks storing beaded bags in plastic is ingenious!

Xiomara will be labeling her party dishes well before the party, Cousin Michelle waves off her loved ones until she can't see them down the street, Merisa's girls are wearing the same color top and bottom to look taller (except no beige), Cousin Thierry will be telling his girls not to shave their legs before a date, Kevin will save a lot of money on gas knowing he never has to drive the Pizanos in his two-door car, and Cousin Mimi thankfully cut the front yard just before the rain yesterday leaving the back undone and unsightly.

This is all fabulous and encouraging news except that The Joan is just slightly annoyed because she thinks I will become rich and famous after publishing The Joan Chronicles and her Pearls (for her posthumously), and I will travel the world and have the fun without her. I reminded her that it won't be as much fun to travel the world without her physically but she will be there in spirit and if she really wants me to be happy she could maybe do some sort of angel maneuver to make sure I do become rich (famous is not necessary and actually undesirable).

Roy is busy with his Joanie-Honey-Do-List that we never actually showed him, so as things are accomplished, we just add more tasks at the end. Look—the guy likes to be busy, we're just helping him out. Everyone needs to be needed. And if you don't hear from me tomorrow it's because I will be in a full body cast from weeding... I mean gardening. I can confirm now that you do use every muscle group in your body when you weed, even abs!... unless I'm doing something wrong.

The Joan is ending the day not with dinner and a movie but with a brewsky and a movie, and lifts up her glass to you... her Collection.

JOANIE'S PEARL
"Keep shower doors open when not in use to prevent mold and mildew build up."

With Love...

* * *

When my dad first started teaching at the local community college, he was very involved with the Cultural Affairs department and was asked to direct a production of "The Mikado." During the auditions, a Franciscan monk by the name of Father Peter Chepaitis sang "A Wandering Minstrel," and blew everyone out of their seats! As the story goes, someone leaned over and whispered in my dad's ear, "That #&%$@* can SING!". Apparently, Father Peter's mother was a huge fan of "The Mikado" so he knew all the songs very well. To boot, he has the voice of an angel—a truly anointed singer.

Father Peter is not your typical clergyman—he is very relatable so everyone took to him and he made close friends while living in the Borscht Belt. Several years later Father Peter moved and we didn't see him for many, many years. But there are some souls who need no physical connection to stay emotionally close. Father Peter was one of those people for my parents.

When my mom called and asked him to officiate at her Event, he didn't hesitate to say that he would if at all possible, and then made a trip to see her. His ministry partner is Sister Anna, who travels with him, so she joined us for lunch as well. It was a very special and moving reunion, complete with amazing a cappella entertainment with good-for-your-soul harmony by the Father and the Sister.

* * *

Sunday, May 13, 2012 11:08 AM
TJC #66

Happy Mother's Day to all you mothers!! And especially to our new mothers on the list—Nicole and Xiomara—celebrating their first with Jack and Carolina, respectively!! You'll remember Carolina from The Joan

Chronicles past—she was the one mortified that her cat was about to inhale her newly discovered cereal and funny enough, Nicole reports the same problem with her (very fat) cat and Jack's cereal! I think it's meant to be, so am working on the details of that arranged marriage.

It's a beautiful, warm, sunny day here in Hurleyville, NY—an alarming yet welcome sign of global warming. The Joan just attended mass (in the TV room) and is now enjoying a show with Roy on Animal Planet about a corgi who knows when his diabetic owner's blood glucose is too high. She was not surprised and was explaining to Roy that animals' gifts are really not utilized enough. We will now be preparing The Joan for sunning and I'm hoping she will lounge in the newly established "grill circle." Since it's Mother's Day, we won't make her grill anything for us.

Joanie and me sunning on the porch. She wanted
me to cover her mediport with my hand

Friday was a sleep day and The Joan slept an entire shift from 11 AM to 7 PM. We then sort of watched a movie, some of it with "our" eyes closed. Breakfast was nice and early at 3 AM but we also found out at that time that we had no water! I am here to tell you that when you turn on the faucet and there is no water, you instantly really miss it. A pot of warmed up water from the fridge was enough for The Joan to accomplish her French Bath, though, so no fear, The Joan was clean while the rest of us remained dirty, until late afternoon when the water started to flow again.

Some of you know Father Peter, who lived here in the early 70s and officiated at Kaye's "Event." The Joan wants him to do the same so he came down for a visit yesterday.

It was great to see him after 40 years! We had an amazing visit, communion and anointing. (Father Peter says you can never be anointed too much so keep that in mind.)

In closing and as a special Mother's Day surprise I will tell you The Color of the Day: Rose.

JOANIE'S PEARL

"Make sure to remove dead flowers from your blooming plants so those important nutrients and water can be diverted to keep the healthy parts thriving."*(Editor's note: This could also be used as a metaphor for life.)*

With Love...

* * *

Tuesday, May 15, 2012 5:27 PM
TJC #67

Hello Dear Loved Ones,

The Joan had a pretty good day today but sadly, is really unable to eat anything in the last several days without getting sick. Although she is growing weaker, I think the electrolytes and glucose in her IV fluids are really making a difference. Most days, she is getting dressed and coming downstairs, and Sunday she surveyed her Kingdom on foot! Ra has done an amazing job with the yard and the grass is greener than ever. We are almost ready for the Better Homes and Gardens shoot but there is still some (a lot) more planting to be done. Here is an unauthorized photo snapped of The Joan fishing out some garbage from the mini pond/natural spring on our property. I was napping at the time but grateful that Sergie was there to spot her to make sure she didn't go in head-first and contaminate her mediport and/or lose the $4,000 morphine pump in the swamp... I mean "natural spring".

Joanie retrieving unsightly garbage from the stream in our yard

Today, her sister Jane, brother George, niece Michelle and sister-in-law Teddy visited from Minersville. The Joan didn't feel up to getting dressed so wore her dressy pajamas—very fancy. We took a stroll down memory lane and watched VHS tapes of Super 8s that The Joan had transferred. They were from the mid-40s when The Joan was a little girl, to the mid-60s when Ra and I were little. There was even footage of me in a white wooden highchair at my first birthday party. Funny, because putting that highchair back together was on Roy's Joanie-Honey-Do-List (JHDL) and he just completed it yesterday! It's now a plant holder but really fun for Roy to see the high chair in action with me in it proving that it must be a very valuable antique.

And speaking of Roy, he really outdid himself for The Joan this Mother's Day and put us all to shame! Here's the back-story: In approximately 1987, the closet doors in the master bedroom fell off the track (not sure how that's possible, but I digress...). So The Joan went out and purchased all the proper equipment for Sergie or someone handy to replace the closet doors and there they sat in the attic hallway for the last 25 years for some unknown and currently unexplained reason!!! I knew the absence of the closet doors was a thorn in The Joan's side so I put it as the number one priority on the JHDL. "If you do nothing else," I told my beloved, "pppleeeease fix those stupid doors!!!" So off Roy and Sergie went to the Home Depot to purchase all the necessary equipment that was already sitting in the attic hallway (which reminds me of one of Sara's Pearls: Nothing is obvious to the uninformed). And... drum-roll...

Roy fixed the closet doors in a matter of minutes with the pre-existing equipment so the newly purchased equipment can now be returned for full refund. Here's the proof, and do not adjust your dial kids—yes, the closet doors are wallpapered!

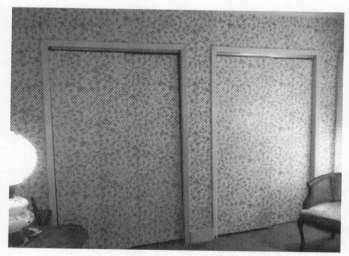

Master closet doors

JOANIE'S PEARL

"When you have cancer, wear earrings so nobody knows you're sick."

With much love...

* * *

Friday, May 18, 2012 11:59 AM
TJC #68

Hello Dear Ones,
The Joan is pretty much sticking to her overall peak day/valley day schedule. Thankfully, our dear friend Millie arrived on a peak day yesterday. The Joan added Millie and her husband to the Collection while Snow-birding in the late 90s when they met as neighbors in Reddington Beach, Florida. Millie is a master gardener and maintains a beautiful pool

for all kinds of wild birds! (Not on purpose, mind you, but the birds love to swim in her pool right on the Intracoastal.) Millie is also a marathon runner and I know Sergie will want me to make sure I tell you that Millie WON the Disney Marathon recently in her age group (let's just say "65 and over").

So Millie arrived yesterday and the weather was magnificent. In honor of her visit, The Joan took an hour break from her IV fluids so they could tour the property. Too bad for Millie, she arrived after the daffodils and before the rhododendron bloomed. Which reminds me of the amazing survival story we had to tell Millie since she is a fellow cat person:

107 Main used to have some sort of cat pheromones oozing from it and we always seemed to have cats adopt us on a serial basis. Several years ago, maybe 10 now, Morris, a cute intact male orange kitty, adopted us. The Joan adored Morris and confided in him on all topics large and small, however, Serge was adamant that they would no longer allow any pets in the house (gasp!).

Anyway, finding testicles on an outside cat unacceptable, and even though I was a licensed vet in Florida, I had to take Morris to the licensed vet in NY to be neutered. Fine. There was only one scheduling snafu and that was that we had tickets to the Forestburgh Playhouse that night (think "Lincoln Center meets the Catskill backwoods"). I didn't want to leave him at the vet's office overnight so inspected the upstairs bathroom calculating how much it would cost me to replace everything should he completely trash it. So we snuck Morris past Sergie and set him up in the upstairs bathroom snug as a bug in a proverbial rug, or so we thought.

We enjoyed the show (no major celebrities spotted) and came home anxious to check our precious patient. O-M-Double-G! The window that had been cracked an inch was open all the way. The screen was sliced in an L shape like Puss from Shrek would have done. And here's the heart stopper: no Morris!!!! Joanie and I were inconsolable running around outside like maniacs, driving the cars in the back yard so we had light—thinking we would find his limp lifeless body—it was a horrible night and no Morris. Joanie and I wore black and dark glasses for two days as we continued to keep food out for him should he make his way home.

Forty-eight hours later, that damn cat was at the front door with not a scratch on him, acting as if nothing happened, and super ready for a tuna steak! What a celebration that was! But Sergie's announcement was the kicker: "Any cat who jumps from the second floor and survives has full rein of the house!".

That night Morris slept under the covers with me with his head on the pillow, and I swear I saw him wink at me. And they say cats don't have the ability to plan? I beg to differ. Anywho, Morris, now Calvin, is the love of my aunt Helen and uncle Morty's life and lives extremely happily spoiled rotten in Brooklyn! My very long winded point: he bounced off the rhododendron and that's why he was uninjured! So the rhododendron remains as a living shrine to Morris to this day. The End.

So The Joan had a fabulous day with Millie yesterday and even took a road trip to downtown Hurleyville to deliver Millie to Sanivan, the spa-slash-B & B operated by our friends Saniye and Ivan, where Millie stayed. We're so thankful that The Joan was having a good day because Millie just flew up overnight to see The Joan. Now that's love!

Last night, though, things took a turn for the worse and The Joan has been in bed with a lot of pain. She has needed a lot of morphine and drugs to keep her comfortable and we are waiting for the hospice nurse to come increase her demand dose. Remember that The Joan is on a constant and low dose of morphine but when she feels very painful she can pump another dose, called the "demand dose." It's taking two-to-three to make her comfortable so she agreed to have that dose increased so that will be happening shortly.

Thank you for your prayers—please continue.

JOANIE'S PEARL
"Horizontal stripes are not flattering on any body type!"

Much Love...

Morris's lifesaving rhododendron

* * *

Sunday, May 20, 2012 5:26 PM
TJC #69

Hello Dear Friends and Family,

The Joan had a lovely day yesterday as we entertained Joyce-the-Nurse from Sloan-Kettering and her husband, Tom, for lunch and completed the Japanese item exchange. Several more major deals were sealed along with whatever Sergie could fit in their car (he may have even snuck some things in the glove compartment as well). Downsizing is in full swing here at 107 Main so consider bringing your own boxes and bubble wrap if you should visit, and be forewarned... you may even leave with things you don't want!

This morning The Joan was up attending mass at 8 AM, dressed and ready for the day, shocking even herself with her energy level. Not many calories are being consumed lately so I thank God every day for IV glucose, potassium and magnesium.

I wasn't sure what The Joan might have up her sleeve as she was very fancily dressed in her beige sweater, beige pants, beige socks and beige slippers. Why she looked almost 5' 2"!

Rosie stopped by in the morning and the three of us had a rousing game of Rummikub on the back deck (we let Rosie win). The weather is magnificent here today so The Joan decided we should road trip to Monticello to buy geraniums. I have to research now how to plant a plant since I mostly just rip things out of the ground—my particular area of expertise. (I also excel in the mulching category.)

So The Joan has been snoozing since we've been home and she is now caught up on the chronicles and I am still alive to talk about it, so that's a relief.

JOANIE'S PEARL

"Put clothes in the dryer only until dry—otherwise you will have static cling issues."

Much Love...

CHAPTER 16

Wednesday, May 23, 2012 7:30 PM
TJC #70

Hello Dear Ones,
Since we last chronicled, we have held steady to the good hours/bad hours schedule with absolutely no ability to predict what the next hour will bring. The Joan has been an early bird, dressed and downstairs before 8 AM—before even me and her IV fluids!
Yesterday she was not nauseous at all and gave Nana the credit for that. It marked the first year anniversary since Nana went to Glory and as always, we felt her presence as strong as ever. Everyone should strive to be half as loved as Nana and The Joan in their lives. At the risk of sounding like a Miss America contestant, there truly would be world peace—I'm certain of it!
The good news is that The Joan has been wanting to eat and enjoying my grilled tofu (marinated in fresh ginger, soy sauce, a little vino and some good olive oil) with strained peanut sauce (see recipe section at end). The bad news is that it may have been a little too much with the mashed potatoes and ice cream chaser. When you're hungry, you're hungry and you don't care about the consequences at the time. Unfortunately, there were consequences if you know what I mean.
And now, boys and girls, it's time for the (true) story of the two plants that fell in love at 107 Main:
The Walking Stick and the Variegated Weigela—A Love Story
Once upon a time, in a far, far away place in the boonies that you won't find with your GPS, a lady named The Joan planted a Walking Stick.

Sara Pizano, MA, DVM

The Joan loved all her plants and regularly celebrated (and documented) their growth. She was also troubled if they didn't reach their full potential and would try a variety of Martha Stewart tricks to keep them healthy.

Sadly, the Walking Stick was a sickly underachiever and barely grew. Then one day, for no known, particular or specific reason, The Joan planted a tiny Variegated Weigela a few feet from the Walking Stick. Then, one other day after that, The Joan noticed that the Walking Stick was growing! Only that one side of the stick was growing and only <u>one</u> branch was growing and reaching out to the Variegated Weigela!

Could it be? A botanical love story? The Joan couldn't believe it and even though the Variegated Weigela was also an underachiever, The Joan decided that the couple should move to their own place of honor on the estate <u>but</u> they, of course, would have to move together and can't possibly be separated since they are the Hepburn-Tracy, the Astaire-Rogers, the Brangelina of 107 Main.

Please see picture below that has not been Photoshopped! And since we all previously accepted that I have limited computer abilities and Roy deserted me and went back to Miami, I will forward a close up for your scrapbook in a separate email.

Proof of botanical love story

JOANIE'S PEARL

"Write items you need at the grocery store on a list in the order they are placed in the store. This will make shopping faster and more efficient."

(Prequel Pearl for those who need it: Always make a list for the grocery store and stick to it!)

Much Love...

* * *

Tuesday, May 29, 2012 8:21 PM
TJC #71

Hello Everyone!
The Joan has been doing well...uncannily well, as a matter of fact. Our schedule of alternating an activity day with a rest day has been working out, as has the new menu of strictly pureed foods or liquids, with the G-tube left open. Attached is an action shot of The Joan from Sunday pruning her Mother's Day petunias (given to her before I found out she doesn't like petunias—oh well, it's the thought that counts!).

Joanie pruning

Ra and I have been super busy with the yard and gardening—still a work in progress. The Joan thought the property looked so good that she said, "We should have a party!". So we did! For Memorial Day, Susan, Ken and Kevin joined us for a cookout and it was a beautiful day from start to finish.

JOANIE'S PEARL
"After clipping woody stemmed flowers, such as lilacs, for your home, hammer the stems so the water is absorbed through them more efficiently and they last longer."

With lots of love...

* * *

Saturday, June 2, 2012 10:57 AM
TJC #72

To Our Dearest Dearests,

I realize I have been remiss in my duties as your correspondent; however, I have two very, very good excuses. It is now monsoon season here at 107 Main and I have been attempting to complete the major spring awakening prior to the building of the arc. It has not been easy but I am almost done with the major parts and will then document the Garden Tour 2012 (tickets are free of charge) for you in photos. In any event, by the end of the day, I am ready for a body cast since, alas, my bones are no longer in Olympic competition shape, if you know what I mean.

Excuse #2 is that The Joan has requested my presence on two road trips this week! The first was on Wednesday to the Home Depot to purchase a fan—that only The Joan could choose—to sit on top of the refrigerator. (Heaven forbid a black one was purchased!)

On Thursday, the Minersville family joined us for another lovely visit. When they left at 3 PM, The Joan took a snooze and kept right on snoozing until 7 AM Friday morning! She did wake up at 11:30 PM on Thursday night, only to announce that she would be up the rest of the night, only to fall asleep again until Friday morning! The fan and the family proved to be quite the events and a recovery period was in order. This is why (in case you have an app to track The Joan's schedule) as House Manager I schedule visits every <u>other</u> day.

Yesterday was road trip #2 to purchase something to provide more shade on the deck. This decision occurred only after days of lengthy discussions with vendors, friends, and family votes, and in the end, a tent-type apparatus was purchased at the Home Depot to cover the whole deck. If you visit, no need to bring sunscreen, as you will be properly shaded.

The Joan has had a rough morning beginning at 5:30 AM, so fell back to sleep and is still in bed. But she has insisted that Serge return to the gym, regardless of her own condition, for his own "mental and physical" health. He is pumping some iron right about now or in a Zumba class shaking his groove thing (just kidding, I know he's not in Zumba because he went once and said it was like stripper moves and not for him).

Serge may have been a little hesitant to return to the gym since it has proved at times to be too humbling. Whilst doing leg curls one day, *his gym-buddies/lady-friends, Yenta and Etta (names changed to protect the innocent) watched on.*

"Wow! Look at Serge's calf muscles! They are really cut!" Yenta said to Etta, super impressed and maybe drooling a little. Serge overheard this conversation so was obviously puffed up, head unable to fit through a standard sized doorway. But then... oh then... the knife! Etta replied, "Yeah... it's just too bad he can't do anything about that stomach!" Cut to the heart! Serge will never be the same. Like I said... humbling... you have to be prepared for those types of things.

10:56 AM update: The Joan is up and ready for the day but considering staying in her jammies—dress is TBA.

JOANIE'S PEARL
"Use deodorant, never antiperspirant."

Much, much love...

* * *

I realize that family members and friends have minimal control over their loved one's attitude when they have a terminal illness, but I can tell you that it is infinitely easier when your loved one is unafraid. My mom was sort of the other end of the spectrum from the fear of death. She had lists and things to complete and goals before she left. So while facing death on this earth, she prayed that God would grant her enough time to complete her to-do lists. She was amazed that He answered her prayers and then some.

It's also nice when your loved one takes the time to plan details that would otherwise be left up to the family or a specific family member. Dealing with those things, at least for me would have been unbearable.

* * *

Wednesday, June 6, 2012 8:16 PM
TJC #73

Hello Dear Friends, Family, Add-ons, Distant Relatives and anyone else not in one of those categories who is reading this,

The word of the week is: "Projects!" And the question is how many projects can The Joan accomplish in one week? (Answer: Unknown since projects are ongoing and are blending together for this reporter).

Overall, The Joan is doing well, and pain/nausea remain episodic. It's been very cold (by my definition) and rainy, so no recent trips touring the estate lately. The Joan is still wearing long johns (top and bottom) under her daily wear and finding it a challenge to stay warm with no body fat.

She continues to be annoyed by the limitations imposed by the IV pole and all the accouterments, so the two of us have developed a lovely habit of waking up at 5:30 or 6 AM, starting her first bag of fluids then returning to Snoozeville. By 10 AM or so, she "takes a break" after the first bag and then is released to go to (1) the attic (2) the cellar (3) Home Depot (4) All of the above or combination thereof. The Joan is very happy with this new tweak to the schedule and feels that she is "getting a lot done". Phew!

We are also making progress with Project eBay, thanks to Kevin. All you ladies who may need a nice full-length dress that The Joan describes as a Ginger Rogers gown, or an orchid floral, sizes 8 and 10 P respectively, if you act now, she may give you a good deal. Also, to be posted soon is The Joan's beloved 4'-deep x 15'-diameter aboveground pool. Take that as a direct hint (Susan) to purchase the pool for your grandchildren (Susan).

Now today you are getting a special Pearl with an action shot attached—lucky you!

JOANIE'S PEARL

"Since shades often rip at the bottom, simply take your handy dandy yardstick," *(the one you use now to clean under the refrigerator)* "and fold the plastic to the desired length over the yardstick to make sure it's straight. Cut the damaged part off and secure seam with double sticky tape." *(Refer to the attached picture of The Joan in action for exact process.)*

Sara Pizano, MA, DVM

Editor's note: *We apologize, but at this time, The Joan has declined being filmed for a How-to You Tube video.*

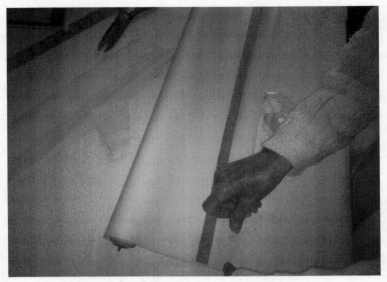

Joanie repairing ripped shade

With Love...

CHAPTER 17

Thursday, June 14, 2012 10:22 AM
TJC #74

Hi Everyone,
　The Joan is hanging in there but having some tough days and struggling with weakness (i.e., extreme "laziness") and an increase in the frequency of vomiting. Being nauseous definitely puts a damper on your day. With intestinal obstructions there isn't a drug that will 100 percent prevent it, but we now have five different drugs that can be given via all different routes, but....
　The good news is that The Joan feels she accomplished all the major items on her list! Strange because Roy's Joanie-Honey-Do-List seems to be getting longer instead of shorter, but I guess those are bonus items.
　Roy arrived on Sunday and got right to work posting the pool on Craig's List, fixing the wicker sofa that was falling apart, reassembling book shelves, soaping wooden drawers, etc., etc. Unfortunately, his mom who just celebrated her 90th birthday, is now in ICU in critical condition and failing, so Roy had to leave for NJ yesterday. Please keep our families in your prayers—we are having a rough week to say the least.

JOANIE'S PEARL
　"Put pillows and stuffed animals in the dryer for 20 minutes periodically to keep them clean."

Much, much love...

* * *

Roy and I met in Miami, Florida in 2006. He is originally from a small town in New Jersey and grew up only two-and-a-half hours from 107 Main. Ironically, as a child he summered just a half an hour from 107 Main in Wurtsboro, where his grandfather owned a summer house. It was a blessing to have our moms so close so that when he flew from Miami he could visit both. During the time when our moms were both failing, I marveled at God's good grace. How amazing that they were so close geographically! It would have made things infinitely harder to have one on each coast.

Roy's mom, Sylviette, was losing her hearing, and hearing aids were not always helpful; her vision was diminishing and she continued to grow weaker. It was a huge struggle to convince her to stop driving (how she was able to get that walker in the trunk, we will never know), even family members failed and were temporarily disowned for trying. She always made sure to fix all the dents and scratches in the Toyota before we visited.

It took her police officer neighbor, while watching her try to pull out of the garage, to get her to hand over the keys. So she struggled greatly while losing more and more of her independence and ability to do the things she loved. Getting old is not for the weak, that's for sure.

It was Thursday, June 14, and I felt strongly called to go to New Jersey to see Sylviette in the hospital. She was critical at the time but I was so torn over leaving my mom. I desperately wanted to be with my mom when she passed, and worried about her if I left. I left the house for New Jersey crying. I turned around after speaking to Roy a few minutes later—I was just too afraid to leave my mom.

The next day, Sylviette's condition worsened so I decided to drive down and kiss her good bye. She was in terrible shape, with heart and organ failure. She was not able to communicate anymore, and the doctors only spoke of keeping her comfortable. We knew it wouldn't be long.

I arrived at the hospital about 2 PM and kissed her hello. Sylviette opened her eyes and Roy said she had not done that in days—I am certain she knew it was me and Roy was amazed. I told her it was OK to go, that her family would be OK and she should let go now. I left a few hours later so upset because I felt she was suffering and knew that is exactly what she did not want at the end. I cried the whole way home.

At 11:30 that night, I was in bed praying that God would take her Home. Praying that her suffering would end, and yes, even begging God. That moment, while I prayed my hardest and deepest, the phone rang and Roy told me that Sylviette had just passed. Praise be to God. I was so relieved for her—she was in Heaven.

* * *

Monday, June 18, 2012 11:20 AM
TJC #75

Hello Dear Ones,
Things are not going well so I wanted to send a quick update. My mom is much weaker and while we help her get around, she was alone in the bedroom for a minute the other day, fell and hit her head on the chaise. Thankfully there was no blood and she bounced just like Nana did when she fell. It scared her enough to abide by the new rule of "mandatory escorting" (before that she insisted she was fine). Yesterday it was hard for her to get out of bed but she wanted to sit in the TV room upstairs so that's where she spent her day. By nighttime, she was extra exhausted and for the second or third time was seeing things we could not.
These things happen towards the end of life on Earth. When she asks me who the other people in the room are, I just tell her that she is blessed to see them but we are not. She thinks that is a good answer and I personally believe it. She slept through the night and seems to be more coherent this morning (enough to tell Sergie he needs a hearing aid) but very, very weak with barely enough energy to speak. This is the "next level," as typically after a good night's sleep she has more energy in the morning but that's not the case today. Kevin asked me "Which level? Up or down?" and I said "Up... closer to Heaven."
I went to NJ on Friday to see Roy's mom for the day. I left at 6 PM and she passed away just before midnight. Sylviette had just turned 90 years old and had a rich life, married to the love of her life for over 50 years and raised three amazing people. She had a great life but really struggled the last couple of years. We are on our way to her funeral now and I will be going home later today. As weak as my mom was yesterday, she was still mortified that she didn't send a card, and made me promise to buy flowers for the family, which I dutifully did this morning.

Sara Pizano, MA, DVM

Sorry I don't have better news for you all but remember my advice about being grateful—I promise it will really help you.
Xo, with love...

* * *

Keeping my mom's treatments organized was essential. It's so easy to forget one thing or the other if you don't keep track of it in some way. She was on multiple medications and bandage changes and I came up with an Excel spreadsheet that worked really well for us. We kept it on the refrigerator so the whole family could refer to it easily.

It also included any doctor's appointments or visitors scheduled so we could stay as organized as humanly possible. The key to being organized is having a simple, easy to use system! Being Type A and having OCD are a great help as well.

* * *

Thursday, June 21, 2012 11:32 AM
TJC #76

Hi Everyone,
The Joan was strong enough yesterday to wash up, get dressed and come downstairs with her eyes open! Still annoyed at, and baffled by, her "laziness" and lack of activity, she went for a jaunt in the yard with Serge and made it to the infamous Grill Circle to sun. Apparently, she expended a lot of energy on the jaunt because then proceeded to sleep an hour and a half in the Grill Circle (I think it has some magical meditative powers because there are no corners).

She's dressed now and making her way downstairs. We seemed to have found the perfect combination of drugs (5 to be exact) that seem to be controlling her nausea and vomiting. The Joan now gets a gel applied to the inside of her wrist every four hours and we then wrap it up like a ham sandwich with plastic cling. It's a combination of three drugs that get absorbed through the skin (called transdermal). She still gets the Zofran intravenously and we also added a Scopolamine patch behind the ear. For all you cruisers, that's the anti-seasickness patch you get in your welcome package. That patch is changed every three days on the same day as the Fentanyl patches (the ones for pain).

Now that spring has arrived and we continue to be responsible for the sustenance of all local wildlife regardless of nature's abundance, we have added a hummingbird feeder.

Coincidentally, the hummingbird nectar needs to be changed every three days like the Fentanyl and Scopolamine patches. The nectar change was added to The Joan's Excel spread sheet that tracks all things going into or on her body, and she was delighted they were all on the same schedule so we would remember to change everything on time. Hopefully nobody will try to administer the hummingbird nectar to The Joan, although it does have a lot of sugar in it so maybe I'm onto something!

And finally, thank you for all your kind words for Roy. He really appreciates it and is at peace that his mom is no longer suffering. Her funeral was truly amazing and her family spoke so eloquently about her life. They were moments I'll never forget. Sylviette's younger sister told a story that will give you an idea of "Syl." It must have been the late 1930s or early 1940s at a time when people (like their father) believed children should be married in chronological order, from oldest to youngest. Barbara's then-boyfriend, Hal, apparently unaware of this rule, went to the house to ask her father for her hand in marriage. Since Sylviette wasn't married yet, it was out of the question for Barbara to get married at that time. Somehow, Syl's dad was tipped off ahead of time and just before Hal arrived, the father went to bed. It was 1 PM and he was not sick.

Learning of this, Syvliette burst into her father's bedroom and scolded him, in no uncertain terms, telling him to get dressed and get downstairs and give his blessing to Hal so he could marry Barbara. So he did and they did and they have been happily married ever since!

Roy's sister also spoke and told the story of the first African American family to move into Little Silver, NJ, in the early 1960s—a solidly white community. The family was tormented, harassed and even had death threats. So Sylviette baked a cake and sent her 10-year-old daughter to their doorstep to welcome them to the neighborhood.

The two families became lifelong friends and Roy's sister reflected at what an incredibly smart decision her mother made, though scary for her at the time. Roy's brother spoke of a "life well lived," and that it was. At the time I didn't know it but the service was recorded so The Joan *and Serge were able to listen to the service yesterday on the Internet. The Joan really appreciated that because she wished she could have been there. Roy will be here tomorrow for the weekend so we're looking forward to having him so he can relax and unwind working on the Joanie-honey-do-list. He just loves being with us in Hurleyville.*

In closing, I also wanted you to know that as weak as The Joan has been, she is still spitting out Pearls. This one is from yesterday:

JOANIE'S PEARL

"When microwaving, stand at least three feet away so you avoid those damaging waves." *(She also wants you to know NOT to put the microwave above the stove because then the damaging waves go directly into your brain.)*

With Love...

CHAPTER 18

Tuesday, June 26, 2012 9:41 PM
TJC #76

Dear Friends, Family, Friends of Friends, Family of Friends and anyone else The Joan Chronicles is being forwarded to,

Since we last left you, there have been many ups and downs and ins and outs and, come to think of it, a 42-degree difference in the ambient outside temperature. Last week The Joan was strategizing the placement of air conditioner units at 107 Main and this morning we had to turn the heat on! My head is spinning.

Overall, we have been able to decrease the number of vomiting episodes from one-to-two per day to one-to-two per week so that's definitely good. Unfortunately, The Joan needed more pain control so once again the oncologist approved an increase in the morphine dose that she can pump. Most days, The Joan is able to get dressed and come downstairs but today was a jammie day spent in bed as those tasks are getting more exhausting to accomplish.

We also had a hospital bed delivered and it is now fashionably set up in the sunroom for daytime snoozes that can sometimes exceed the number of hours in a regular work day. There is a small mattress over the mattress that fills with air in different places at different times so the pressure on the body changes to prevent bedsores. It looks quite comfy and I plan on napping on it when The Joan is not using it... or come to think of it, even if she is... I don't take up much space.

But The Joan feels weaker now and when our hospice Nurse, Padma, told her she was an inspiration, she replied, "I'm done being an inspiration... I'm tired." From her lips to God's ears... she is still working on her list. Roy was able to spend the weekend with us before flying back to Miami this morning and was hard at work as the List Assistant.

Truly, there is an inherent design flaw in the placement of the bird feeders so it is not his fault that the squirrels are using the prevent-a-squirrel-baffle to sit on while feasting on the birdseed in the adjacent feeder. In any event, it took the squirrels a few days to figure the whole thing out so we still saved approximately $5.28 during that span of time.

JOANIE'S PEARL
"When cutting a round birthday cake, cut straight across and then cut slices perpendicular to the first cut—it's less mess and yields more pieces."

Much Love...

* * *

Sunday, July 1, 2012 4:08 PM
TJC #77

Hello Dear Ones,

Well, we seem to be at another level now. Since the hospital bed was delivered, The Joan has pretty much been in it. To her delight it isn't too intrusive in the sunroom and the dining table has remained in the same place so there is still plenty of room for people to sit (one of her many concerns about "the bed"). This is a similar phenomenon to Billy Crystal's "It's not how you feel, it's how you look," but thankfully, comfort has prevailed.

The Joan has great difficulty walking now but did make it to the bathroom this morning with bilateral spotters. Having arrived in the lavatory wobbly and weak, she demanded the yardstick. I had no idea why and filled with fear knowing that it was not in the location it has been since 1971. Uh oh... we had to confess it wasn't there.

"Then get me the measuring tape!!" And then The Joan proceeded to measure the width of the downstairs bathroom since she recently learned that by code it has to be a certain width. Double Uh oh—it wasn't done to code and she fretted that we may have to remove it before the house sells.

What I haven't told you before is that back in January, The Joan decided that she would give into Sergie's 25-year desire to move to Florida, and asked for an appraisal on 107 Main. But the realtor wasn't scheduled before her illness took a turn for the worse so it was postponed. We then successfully talked her out of getting the appraisal even though it was on her list of things to accomplish, to make it easier on us after she leaves for Heaven. We all know The Joan, and any number a realtor concludes will be $1 to $2 million short in her opinion. So... she just had to measure the bathroom and I can only conclude it's because she's a worry junkie.

So we are bracing ourselves and panicking intermittently for good or bad reasons. Today The Joan told us "it won't be long" and I'm doing my best to prepare all of you, but I suppose none of us will really ever be ready. She sometimes is in a semi-sleep state but talks like she's awake. Yesterday she said, "If they made marijuana legal in NY, it would be much better for the state." At the time, I thought she was reading/commenting on the Julie Andrews memoir, Home, that was in her hands. Now I do not confess to be an expert in all things Julie Andrews but found it odd that Ms. Andrews, a Brit, might give commentary on legalizing pot in New York State.

When I looked at The Joan she opened her eyes and said, "I think I was dreaming". (PS: in case The Joan Chronicles are being passed along to anyone affiliated with the Drug Enforcement Agency, please note "dreaming" in the last sentence, and refer to earlier chronicles whereby we decided we did not want to give The Joan the munchies so never placed an order for the Mary Jane as a method of pain control. Thank you.)

JOANIE'S PEARL
"Never give little children ice cubes in their drinks." (Editor's note: sorry, no age specified.)

Much, much love and thanks...

* * *

Sara Pizano, MA, DVM

Monday, July 2, 2012 9:25 AM
TJC #78

Quick update:
The Joan is up and stronger this AM. In fact, I caught her moving the bird feeder onto the deck (unauthorized and dangerous for sure).

Love...

* * *

Tuesday, July 3, 2012 4:11 PM
TJC #79

Hello to The Joan's Collection,
Today, confused and irritated by the weakness in her legs, The Joan decided it was time to build her leg muscles up so requested the foot bike. See below for proof/action shot! She has also declared that the new hospital bed (from now on to be referred as "the bed") is <u>too</u> comfortable. So comfortable, in fact, that she doesn't want to get out of it!

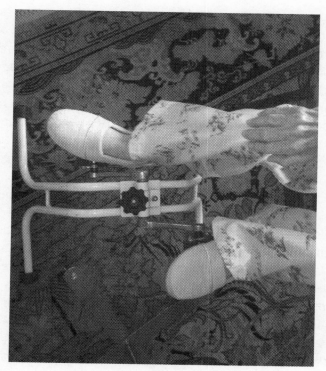

Joanie Tour de France conditioning

The Joan certainly does have a nice setup in the sunroom. As you know, "the bed" goes up, down, inside out, backwards and forwards so you can pretzel yourself into an infinite variety of positions. There is also a mattress on top of the mattress so the air alternates firmness every 15 minutes. In addition to that, we were sent one of those bedside tables that also goes up and down. The Joan keeps all her necessities at close reach—notepad and pen, chewing gum, phone, tissues, etc.—but her favorite part is the bookstand Sergie gave her for her book so she doesn't have to hold it! What a relief—those hardcovers are heavy. (The Joan has thus far been resistant to the Kindle Serge bought her. Some of you know what I'm talking about—we really miss paper.)

Anywho, from her vantage point, she can monitor her kingdom and all her yard pets that now include a tiny newborn fawn. Other regulars include rabbits (and FYI they aren't playing when they jump straight up and down, it's rabbit foreplay), Mr. and Mrs. Woodchuck who reside under the shed, an entire extended family of chipmunks, red squirrels who fit on the "squirrel proof" ledge of the bird feeder, regular size squirrels and a few sightings of bear, fox and coyote. Oh, and the raccoon who I caught red handed at the bird feeder buffet one evening.

Living in the sunroom, you automatically become a crazy bird enthusiast. Serge regularly refers to his bird books (one that actually plays the sound of the particular bird when you press the corresponding number) and has kept track of the type and number of birds he's seen in the yard—76 and counting!

But you don't need a book to figure out the hierarchy of these flying creatures. Blue Jays rule. They are big and fat and loud and God help anyone else at the bird feeder when they are ready for their snack—even if they have fur! Doves are at the other end of the spectrum and never cause a scene—they just go to the ground to eat the fallen seed if there is too much competition.

There's a big huge pine tree right next to the deck and all the birds sort of line up in queue depending on their class status. Cowbirds are team players but only with other cowbirds. I saw them bully a poor little bird right off the branch—twice! There were three cowbirds on one branch and they kept inching the little bird towards the end, like off a plank. Finally, the little bird caught on and went to another branch but @#^% gasp! There were two more cowbirds on the next branch that did the same thing to him!... So off he flew with hunger pains.

I could go on but you get the picture. Sorry, people, there is not much else going on at 107 Main, so we find ourselves engrossed in the daily drama of the bird feeders. And, by the by, don't even think about yelling at the squirrels who eat six pounds of bird feed a day—Joanie has passed The Squirrel Protection Act, and reasons that if we would just buy them peanuts they wouldn't have to eat the bird food! Needless to say, Sergie is mourning his retirement money going up a tree in the cheeks of a squirrel.

Well, dear loved ones, it's another beautiful day. The Joan is snoozing and in an act of solidarity, so is Sergie.

JOANIE'S PEARL

"After stripping, but before varnishing that piece of wood furniture you are refinishing, wipe with alcohol to remove all dust particles. That way, you will end up with a clean and smooth surface."

Much Love...

* * *

Everyone always commented on how strong I was during my mom's illness, but I felt so relieved to be with her and make sure she didn't want for anything. I'm typically an easy crier but for some reason, I kept it together except for a few breakdowns. She knew how painful this was for all of us and I didn't want to make it harder on her by being a waterworks every day. But I think you should feel free to cry once in a while with your loved one, otherwise, they might not think you care!

As we struggled with edema and my mom was sleeping more, I was adamant about preventing bed sores. Not only are they painful but they can lead to large, non-healing wounds and systemic infections. One day, she slept for many hours, though she was still able to move around. The problem was that she didn't, and after a 6 hour nap, there was a blister on her ankle bone.

I burst into tears at the sight of a three-millimeter blister on her little toe! I mean really hysterical. I was supposed to be the responsible one and make sure this didn't happen and I had a tremendous amount of guilt. My family, including my mom and our hospice nurse tried to comfort me. Things like this happen and Type A's like me don't handle it well. That's OK—I'm a Human Type A—it happens to the best of us. It may happen to you and you just have to remember that all you can do is your best.

* * *

Wednesday, July 11, 2012 1:59 PM
TJC #80

Hello Dear Ones,
The Joan is hanging in there but days are much slower moving now. As her disease progresses, it's caused some blockage in her lymphatic system, which causes swelling (edema) in her extremities. We've been

struggling with her feet especially, and the danger is: the more edema, the higher the chance of bedsores that don't heal and of course, are painful and lead to other problems like systemic infections. Because of this, we've been forced to decrease her IV fluids again and are now down to 500 cc a day.

The alternating air mattress on "the bed" was too firm for her fragile and fatless body, so she now has a special foam top that seems to be more comfortable for her. At night, she sleeps pretty soundly, and typically you can hear her breathing. But the other night, I admit, I didn't hear her breathing and panicked. It was dark, so after a few alarming moments, I turned on the light, at which time The Joan awoke (annoyed) and asked "Why did you turn on the light!?" Phew.... "Just looking for something," I responded sheepishly. Snagged!

And The Joan is still grateful for many things—Roy is back with us and working on a variety of projects at once (who knew the hissing sound from the propane tank meant there was a leak?) and my mom says she's lucky to be dying at this time of year because the watermelon is excellent, and is her new vice, replacing the Yuengling. Kevin is our supplier and he always picks the best for The Joan.

We also love the 4th of July so Merisa and I (both Florida residents where fireworks are legal and encouraged) went to the Home Depot for sparklers. Who knew that fireworks were illegal in NY? Not me—apparently The Joan smuggled all those fireworks and sparklers from her home state of Pennsylvania for us growing up. Anywho, Merisa's daughter, Lexi, learning that The Joan wanted illegal sparklers, made them herself—see picture below. If you look closely, you can see the pieces of ziti holding the sticks together, which I will later serve to Sergie for dinner (waste not, want not). What a thoughtful, beautiful and touching gift from Lexi's little hands and big heart!

And the other night, The Joan felt up to watching a movie, so we made the trek to the living room to watch "Dolphin Tale," that Roy sent to us. It's a true and amazing story that we highly recommend. My only advice is to have at least a box and a half of Kleenex per person when you watch it. The Joan loved it and, PS there's a happy ending so you now know that you can watch the whole thing.

Lexi's sparklers for The Joan. Birthday candles are sticking out perpendicular to the sticks that are held together with ziti!

JOANIE'S PEARL

"When flying or picking up a loved one at the airport, always arrive super-early. Especially when flying south to north, the tailwinds often speed up the flight and your loved ones will most likely arrive early."

With Much Love...

* * *

Many of us know that children, when facing a serious challenge, rise up to heights we couldn't possibly imagine as adults. Such as it was with Lexi and Coley. They were very close to my mom and she instilled a trust in them so they knew they could talk to her about anything or ask her any question. And they had questions. Lexi and Coley are highly creative and decided to each write entries in a little book and send it to Joanie in New York from their home in Florida. They asked that she respond in the same book so they would have a keepsake.

Thanks for Being
nice to animals
including Humans.
Love
Lexi

*Some of the entries from Lexi and Coley's memory
book with my mom's response*

are you scared
about Dieing?
It makes me
Sad when I Think
about it.

Love
Lexi

I will never forget
you. I will always
remeber you.
Love
Lexi

Dear Joanie

Thank you for
every Thing you
Done. are you
felling a little Better
I Wonder what
Life would Be Do
without you Do
you Know? I also
Want to, tell you
if you can be my
angle? I hope you
will make lots of

friends In heaven?)
The gift Thanks, for
I love Love you
xoxox

Love
Lex

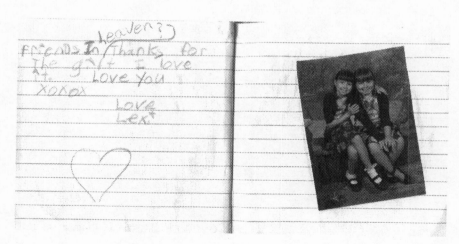

187

Dear Akeyi a Coli, ⑦

There are so many memories of you. All those parties, the dollhouse, riding bikes, Isabel & youboth in the pool a your sliding pool in grama's yard,

Then you asked me a very big important question about dying.

No honey, "I'm not afraid about dying, I've had of about 75 years of a long, happy life. Sometimes we're sad, maybe annoyed. But then it passes & everything is OK again. We just must remember to NEVER to hit anyone. The most important is to keep healthy.

(turn)

You know how to do that by eating what Mom tells you to eat, exercising (you do lots of that), & going to be a sleep on time.

Very important is to spend time enjoy family & friends. When you are nice to people & they are nice to you, you all have fun together. Lots of memories a photos,

I want you to have singing, dancing, feed the animals. memories after I am gone.

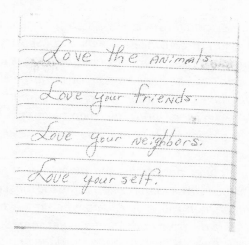

Love the animals.

Love your friends.

Love your neighbors.

Love your self.

Saturday, July 14, 2012 12:51 PM
TJC #81

Hi Everyone,

Yesterday, The Joan walked to the restroom and in honor of our Olympic athletes in training, wanted to walk up two steps just to test herself. She did it, of course, but now most mobilization takes two spotters.

And while the egg crate foam has proved to be more comfortable than the alternating air mattress, it still wasn't luxurious enough. Hearing this, Roy, the engineer, was on the case (remember his Gas-X prescription). He got online and researched bed sore prevention, and found that sheepskin is the absolute best prevention (and just so you know, for dinner party conversation, there is some sort of undisclosed sheep problem in Australia and New Zealand right now). The sheepskin has made a tremendous difference so I am happy to report that that sheep did not die in vain—his skin is helping The Joan's skin stay intact. We also successfully convinced her not to care that she didn't have a sheet over it to keep it ultra clean—a true accomplishment.

Unfortunately, and as expected, The Joan is still struggling with pitting edema, so the IV fluids were cut back again today to 250 cc. This is done to prevent fluid from building up in the lungs, which is obviously very uncomfortable and could compromise her breathing. The feeling of thirst and dehydration is unpleasant but unavoidable.

The Scopolamine patch (the cruise patch for nausea) adds to that feeling of thirst and I'm convinced it was a conspiracy by the cruise industry so people purchased more alcoholic beverages at the bar while mid-ocean. But back to The Joan, today was another day of random thoughts—all the things that are in her brain hibernating. She kind of feels bad that her sister Mary Jane really didn't want the "Mary" in front of her name, but I told her not to worry since everyone just calls her Jane anyway.

She's thinking about her family and memories maybe from many years ago growing up in little Minersville. I think the most classic example of small town America in those days was when my Nana left her first born, George, outside the front door (alone) to get some sun when he was a baby. When she came out, he was gone, carriage and all. When asked decades later if she was concerned she might never see him again she said, "No. I knew whoever took him would bring him back eventually." And they did... it was one of the neighbors who wanted to show the baby to her mom. Now that's Small Town America at its best (disclaimer to you new moms: do not try this at home).

So we're getting much closer to Heaven where The Joan will be healed and please know that you are on this list because The Joan loves you! This is her Pearl from yesterday:

JOANIE'S PEARL
   "In the summer, you shouldn't wear perfume/cologne as it will attract bees."

Much Love...

* * *

One of the hardest things for a caregiver or loved one is to stop giving care or permission for care in the way of medications, food or intravenous fluids. We are hardwired as human beings to live, so it is only natural for us to want to do whatever it takes to keep life going. As my mom's condition deteriorated, she was able to eat less and less. Because she was not able to get out of bed the last few days before she passed, her feet were swelling so the intravenous fluids had to be decreased and ultimately stopped. As a veterinarian, I have often said, "Just because there is a treatment, doesn't make you obligated to do it." If an eighteen-year-old dog has cancer, just because surgery, chemotherapy and radiation therapy are available, does not mean you are a bad pet owner or love your pet any less if you don't pursue those treatments.

But with a loved one, it's still a punch in the gut. It was so difficult to stop the intravenous fluids even though intellectually I knew that the fluids were creating the edema, meaning they were not staying in the spaces necessary, and giving them could ultimately cause fluid in the lungs (called pulmonary edema) and difficulty breathing. Stopping the fluids was really hard for me.

* * *

Monday, July 16, 2012 8:07 PM
TJC #82

Hello Sweet Friends and Family,

Today we have a new normal, as most days seem to present now. The Joan was awake for about two hours this morning and enjoyed part of ABC's "Secret Millionaire" on iPad TV (and I just needed one more reason to cry—bring tissues if you're tuning in to that show... Note to Self: Try "America's Funniest Videos" next time). She's been sleeping since, and we did her bath/change and spa treatments in bed for the first time, but she didn't completely wake up.

The Joan is no longer getting IV fluids, because of the edema, which we have been able to keep under control so far and her lungs are still clear, thankfully. Her occasional pain/soreness seems to be from lying in bed, as opposed to cancer pain, so I took the liberty of giving her a couple of morphine pumps.

So it is with a heavy heart that I write this... but the fly annoying me that I have been trying to kill for three days reminded me of a funny story The Joan told the other day:

In the early 1970s, my Aunt Zizi and cousins Thierry, JP and Cat lived with us for a summer between their move from Illinois to Long Island. The flies in the house were driving The Joan nuts so she announced a contest: She would pay five cents for each dead fly we presented. But as The Joan was shelling out the big bucks left and right for dead flies, she made a scandalous discovery. One of the "entrepreneurial" children intentionally left a door open so more flies would come in for them to kill! The culprit was never identified and the contest called off, but I can tell you it wasn't me and we also cannot ignore the possibility that it could have been an "accident"... we'll never know... another unsolved mystery.

JOANIE'S PEARL

Disclaimer: The Joan typically does not recommend products, but she did want you to know how amazing Scrubbing Bubbles Toilet Gel is. You release this blob of gel from a dispenser that sticks to the inside toilet wall, and each time you flush—voila!—like having a maid.

Much Love and so sorry I don't have better news for you—our hearts are breaking along with yours.

NY Times Correction: The Joan corrected me yesterday... she said wearing perfume/cologne attracts <u>mosquitoes</u>, not bees. Please accept my sincere apologies.

CHAPTER 19

Being a caregiver is not for the weak of heart. You have to be prepared for your loved one to become politically incorrect as time progresses, to tell you their deep, dark secrets or regrets that you may wish you did not hear. They may tell you things about other loved ones that caused them great pain and cause you current pain. The more prepared you are, the better equipped and stronger you will be, so you can be empowered to give loving care to your spouse, parent, child or whoever is terminally ill, without judgment.

I have also found that it is infinitely less hard on the loved ones when the person preparing to pass is not afraid, and when they know for sure they are going to Heaven. The whole thing is hard enough, but panic and fear cast an even darker shadow on the passing.

So if they are not a believer, you should consider spiritual counseling—whatever that means for your loved one. We will all pass and no amount of fear about it will change that. The only thing that can change is how we perceive it. I was blessed that my mom looked forward to Heaven and had more curiosity than anything else. She once asked me, "What do you think I'll do all day in Heaven?" Darned if I know, but it's looking like you'll find out first at the rate we're going, I told her.

I know I have said this before, but it bears repeating: When your loved one is at the end of this life, you are the most important advocate for their comfort. That may mean drugs for pain, anxiety or nausea; what they sleep on, their diet, whatever. It will mean different things for different people. Don't stop asking questions of the medical team or doing your own research on behalf of your loved ones to create the

Sara Pizano, MA, DVM

best environment for them—mentally, emotionally, physically and spiritually.

* * *

Tuesday, July 17, 2012 1:35 PM
TJC #83

Hi Everyone,
The Joan was awake for a little while this morning. At times it was hard to understand her but then she brightened up a little bit. Kevin stopped by and while reading the obits in the paper (his daily ritual), read a part about a man he knew from Grahamsville. He announced that the man was married for 48 years and The Joan said (now mind you, she is not a chatter box these days)... The Joan said, "That's what did him in." The Joan made a funny! Then she had some watermelon and went back to sleep. One thing I can tell you, though, is that The Joan is no longer concerned about being politically correct.
Our other good news is that the second sheepskin arrived and is now under The Joan's legs. Weird that it's dark green—wait for it—I can't not say it... it must have been the green sheep of the family—get it?
And I apologize in advance for the Adams Family-esque Pearl today, but it is what it is....

JOANIE'S PEARL
"Make sure to print your obituary in your local paper <u>after</u> the funeral, not before, lest some unscrupulous thieves get the tip and rob your house during the funeral." *(I can't make this stuff up, folks, from The Joan's mouth to TJC.)*

With much love and thanks...

* * *

Thursday, July 26, 2012 12:25 PM
TJC #84

Hello Dear Ones,

The Joan is resting comfortably as we speak. She credits Roy for the super-comfy sheep skins as they have really made a difference for her. She is surprised (and relieved) that she is not in severe pain at this point, which she kind of anticipated. Thankfully, she is no longer hesitating to use the morphine pump and we had the time interval decreased from ten to five minutes in between pumps as needed. (The Joan declined to have the continuous rate or pump dose increased.)

It's now been 12 days since The Joan has received intravenous fluids, and as you know, the majority of what goes in her mouth goes out into the gastric bag. Her core body is still very strong so I personally am classifying her status as miraculous. I have a call into Vatican City for official confirmation, but it truly defies all rational medical knowledge.

The Joan believes one of us is "holding her back," and not ready to let go, as she didn't expect to take so long to die. We have assured her that we don't want her to suffer and that it's OK. She says she's ready, and "living in the love" from all of you.

I am also taking credit for giving The Joan a big laugh this week. As you probably know, The Joan is not a big laugher but says she's "laughing on the inside." Anyway, we were reminiscing about an old male friend of mine who is super smart, sweet, thoughtful, good looking—perfect catch on paper. One day years ago, he confessed his love for me and when I told The Joan I just didn't feel the same way she pleaded "TRY HARDER—I LOVE HIM!!" We got a good chuckle out of that one.

JOANIE'S PEARL

Always carry some nutritious snacks with you, so when you are out and get hungry you don't make bad food choices.

Much Love...

* * *

Monday, July 30, 2012 7:22 PM
TJC #85

Dear Loved Ones,
The Joan is still with us but has been comatose since yesterday morning, so it won't be long now. I am sorry that I haven't chronicled in

a few days, but as you can imagine it's been heartbreaking and difficult to tell you what's happening. I will spare you details and tell you the important things that will stay with you and are important to you.

I believe that we are keeping The Joan pain-free and comfortable, thanks mostly to morphine, Ativan and sheep.

We are holding her hand 24/7 and sometimes I hold her foot if Ra and Serge each have a hand.

We put the Biotene stuff in her mouth every half hour for dry mouth (as she made us promise we would do when she couldn't, like a million times).

Her hair looks really good and is curly which was her life-long ambition.

And lastly I will leave you with a God story so you know how The Joan is still connecting people, even now:

Our amazing hospice nurse, Padma, was here tonight and said that harp music has been known to calm people as they pass (this is actually a two-part God story, now that I think about it). First, when Merisa was here earlier today she said we should play The Joan some relaxing soft music. Second, Isabelle, age 12 (Zizi's granddaughter and Cat's daughter), plays the harp and asked The Joan recently if she could play at her Event. What are the chances that Padma had a harp CD in the car for The Joan? Still connecting...

And lastly, The Joan feels all your love through miles and time and that's the most important thing.

JOANIE'S PEARL (from the other day)
"Don't wear black when it's hot outside."

Much, much love...

* * *

Tuesday, July 31, 2012 9:21 AM
So sorry

To The Joan's Collection,
Ra and I were holding my mom's hands at 4 AM this morning when she went to Heaven. She was there for our first breath and God allowed

us to be there for her last—what an awesome honor. You were all there too—she felt and we feel your love. So now, your beloved aunt, cousin, sister, friend has become your most trusted angel and we have all been divinely blessed by her heart and her life.

If you live far away and would have to fly to The Event, The Joan doesn't want you to spend "all that money" flying last minute. Of course, you are all welcome and you could try to get a bereavement fare, but please know that The Joan loves you and didn't want you to feel obligated to come.

And lastly, a recount of the most classic "Joan story." I assumed The Joan would want you to make a donation to one of her favorite causes instead of flowers. She responded: "But I _love_ flowers!! Can't they do both??" and I said, "Of course!" So here is my suggestion. Say you were going to spend $40 on flowers...instead, spend $20 on flowers and $20 can go to one of The Joan's causes. It's up to you, again, just a thought.

With much love and grateful hearts, we are so sorry for your loss,
On behalf of The Joan, Serge, Ra and Sara

CHAPTER 20

Tuesday, August 7, 2012 10:45 AM
TJC—The Final Chapter Here on Earth

To The Joan's Collection,
    Thank you to all of you who sent love, cards, flowers, reached out to us, and joined us in the celebration of my mom's life at The Event last week. For those of you who attended the viewing, I know you will agree it was an amazing night—and for me, beyond words. For those loved ones who couldn't make it, I want to tell you about it. It was truly an amazing Celebration..."Viewing" just doesn't describe it in any way, shape or form. Roy said he's never experienced anything like it—the power, the love, the spirit in the room was indescribable.
    Father Peter Chepaitis is the Franciscan Friar who entered our lives in the early 1970s, whom I've spoken about. He has always been very special to my parents although we haven't seen him much in the last many years. It was very important to my mom that he officiate at her Event. So important, in fact, that she had me call him to get his schedule just before she went to Heaven. He visited and had a heartfelt talk with her about who was "in control." That's all fine and good and we can laugh about it now, but The Event occurred when he was available during a narrow window of time, and I can assure you it was no accident!
    Father Peter has an amazing voice and plays the violin beautifully, which he did at the Celebration. Then, my cousin Thierry spoke and gave the most beautiful dedication:

Good evening.

My name is Thierry Murad. I am Aunt Joanie's godson.

Back in the late 1950s, my Mom (Cecile—also known as Zizi) arrived in the United States from her home country of France. She came to America alone (with no family) to marry my father (Paul), whose best friend was Sergio Pizano.

Uncle Sergio's girlfriend (one day to be his wife) was Joan Hahn. Sergio and Joan were the first people my mom met upon her arrival to the States. Little did they all know that this would be the beginning of a 53-year friendship. But it was more than just that.

But before I continue, allow me to give a little background: My family is small. I have one brother; one sister. Most of our family lives overseas... My mom has two sisters who live in France. My father's only brother passed away some 30 years ago and his sister lives in California. So it seemed that somewhere, one day, many years ago, the Pizanos adopted my family (or the Murad family adopted the Pizanos). I'm not sure that we can really date it.

Mrs. Hahn (or Nana) Joan's mom, and Clementina, Sergio's mom, were as much second grandmothers to us as our own grandparents who mostly lived in other countries.

Our cousins, Sara and Rafael, and my siblings grew up together. We attended each other's school and other functions, Thanksgivings and other holidays. More childhood memories than I can count include our families being together. Ra and I spoke about this the other day—we both agreed that there were too many memories to add up.

Of course, it wasn't enough to just be a part of the family in Hurleyville, we had to include Minersville as well. Attending college back in the early 80s in Virginia, whenever I was driving home to New Jersey, I'd try and swing by to see Aunt Jane and all the family. I'm sure sometimes they'd wonder who this kid was showing up at their house claiming to be a cousin or nephew. But all I had to mention was that I was Zizi's son or Aunt Joanie's godson and it meant an instant free meal. Of course the first time I visited their home in Minersville, no one bothered to mention to me what the family business was... but I'll save that story for another time.

So, every December, when I was about to have my birthday...there were two things I could count on:

1)   My Mom would be the first to call me that day... and

2)   I'd have a birthday card in the mail from my Aunt Joanie

I mention this because it didn't matter how old or young we were—for all my life, there was a constant about Aunt Joanie—you knew there was a solution if you wanted it, a suggestion shared, some hint for good health ("don't forget your vitamin C").

Joan was more than just my godmother. She was a second mom to me. An aunt in every respect and then some—not just to me, but to my brother, sister and our children.

These are just words, but to myself, my brother and sister, my parents, and our kids, the influence and effect of Aunt Joan (and Uncle Sergio) on our lives has been more impactful than any other of our actual blood relatives... How did this happen? I don't know...but something about them would make you want to share every dream, every success, every heartbreak, every story.

My wife, Lisa, and I, and my daughters live down South now. Every trip home North has always been the same: we need at least three days: after we visit my mom, do we visit my sister or Aunt Joan first? There was never a doubt, never a question that we'd be making the drive to Hurleyville—the only question was which day would it be and how long could we stay. For we could not wait to go and we always hated to leave.

It's no secret to anyone who knew Joanie that she had an endless stream of energy. Always a task for everyone. Always a project she was finishing and another one in the planning stage. Rafael and I were joking to each other that upon arrival in Heaven, Aunt Joan was probably already re-organizing things up there and likely picking out new wallpaper. Heaven will never be the same, but better for her being there to run things and take care of everyone, the same as she did here on Earth.

Some seven months or so ago the doctors' diagnosis was for her to have only a few months to live, but that wasn't enough time for her to complete her list, so she had to defy the doctors and stick around an extra five months, a reflection of her inner energy, strength and determination—and the tremendous care and love of Sara, Ra, Uncle Sergio, Roy, my mom, Susan, and countless friends and family.

Anyone who was fortunate enough to read Sara's updates these past months got a good glimpse of Aunt Joan's strength and tenacity during this difficult period.

In preparing my comments for today, it occurred to me how many key words and phrases exist which immediately make one think of her:

Vitamins
Prevention magazine
Wallpaper
Yard sale
Japan
Meditation
Dogs, cats, deer...

She loved animals. She loved people. She had a great and contagious laugh (kind of a "HA!") and boundless energy. She loved art, culture. You could discuss almost anything with Aunt Joan.

You never wanted to disappoint her. You always wanted to please her. If Aunt Joan had a plan, you didn't really question it, you just knew you needed to be there.

One year for Thanksgiving, Aunt Joan announced we were going native—for example, Indian Corn and the turkey was probably wild also. No one questioned it, you just knew you were going to eat it and enjoy it.

She was an authority in family health (well, for our family anyway). If someone was sick or in pain, one of us was always sure to say, "Did you check with Aunt Joan?" or "What did Aunt Joan tell you to do?"

This carried over to her daughter Sara, the veterinarian. Although Sara was now living down in Florida, I recall my wife Lisa and I checking with her a number of times regarding the health of our cat. Same questions: "Did you check Sara?" or "What did Sara tell you to do?" (Like mother, like daughter).

I don't recall Aunt Joan ever asking for anything; but she was always giving. She had a way of impacting and affecting people. Perhaps that's why she had so many friends—in the States and abroad. She had this rare gift in which you just wanted to be around her.

When Uncle Sergio and Aunt Joan were living in Toyama, Japan, some years ago, I had the opportunity to visit them a couple of times. It wasn't enough for Aunt Joan to just be in Japan—she found herself teaching English to young children. This is especially impressive knowing that when she arrived there she didn't speak any Japanese. But the impact of their time in Japan is evident by the artwork in their home and the stories still shared.

When thinking about my mom and Aunt Joan, they weren't just the best of friends, they were sisters. It drew them together as well our families. And even with her passing, I know that the bond between our families will always remain.

There are some people referred to as the "rock" of a family or the "matriarch" of a family. In some ways, Aunt Joan was both, I suppose. She certainly drew us together and although she might be gone in body, she remains in spirit and her strength is felt around us.

How very lucky we are that she was a part of our lives; how very special we were to have been blessed by her impact; how fortunate we are that she touched us in so many ways.

Aunt Joan loved us; even if she didn't always say the words. Maybe it's a Pennsylvanian thing?

At the end of a phone conversation, I'd always say, "Love you Aunt Joan"—but she might say, "Well, thanks for calling," or "OK dear," or "Tell Lisa I said hello," or "Bye bye, we'll talk with you soon." But I guess I knew the end was near when in my last phone conversation with her she said, "I love you."

So, I don't know how best to end this, except to say Aunt Joanie, we love you and already we miss you terribly, but we thank you for all that you gave us and did for us.

You will forever be with us and in our hearts...And we'll talk with you soon...

* * *

Next, Sue and Ken Kantor spoke and they had us in stitches. We laughed and cried, sometimes all at the same time. Here's what they said:

Susan:

Our friend Joan was a friend like no one else. Joan was the most compassionate, honest, sympathetic and nonjudgmental person there could be. She was always there for whoever needed her. Joan had a very special talent of being able to express her thoughts on how to eat right and stay healthy, and how things should be done such as gardening, plumbing, electrical jobs and entertaining. Joan had a wonderful skill of giving advice, but it was always said in the most kind, caring, and meaningful way. I do not think that anyone could EVER take offense when Joan expressed her thoughts on how things should be done. Joan was just so special.

Joan's medical advice was always appreciated by everyone that she touched. My daughter told Sara that she and her mother (me) would not have survived if Joan had not given us her advice and help in healing childhood cuts, bruises, illnesses and even poison ivy. When my daughter developed a rash all over a body one summer we went up the hill to visit Dr. Joan, who we always consulted first. Joan, practicing Indian medicine, went out in the fields, picked Jewelweed and squirted the juice onto my daughter's body and BAM the poison ivy was gone. Once when I was not feeling well for a year, and no doctor—not even two NYC specialists—could solve my medical problem, I relented and tried Joan's remedy and immediately the vitamin regiment healed me.

Joan has made an impact on everyone's life and part of her will always be in all of us. The Pearls that Sara wrote in her chronicles are certainly a survival list and a guide of Heloise-type hints that are certainly beneficial to all of us.

Joan died in the beauty that she so appreciated. She died watching the squirrels eat the nuts, the birds eating the seeds and the hummingbirds sipping the nectar. She diligently fed the birds and the squirrels and deer, and when Joan could no longer do it her family continued doing what Joan wanted... protecting and feeding all of the wildlife that lived in her backyard. I remember when Joan stayed up for two nights taking care of a baby bird that fell out its nest, and Joan would feed the bird with a dropper every few hours.

Joan died enjoying the sunroom, watching the hummingbirds eating the sweet nectar that the family filled on the same three-day schedule as Joan's pain patch, and hearing the birds singing their songs. It was because of her enjoyment of nature and the dedication of Serge, Ra and Sara's medical skills—and Sara fighting for what she thought was right—that Joan lived past the doctors' prognosis of life. Then too, Joan, until the very end had a To Do list for Roy and the rest of the family. And she wanted that list to be finished before she left us. Joan's family all pitched in and maintained the yard, just as if it was Joan who was out there doing what she loved best—gardening.

And the family fulfilled all of Joan's lists—making the house, yard, and driveway look as if it was The Joan doing the work. She taught them all well. Sara even learned to garden almost as well as her mother. And now that Joan has given us so much, it is her time to move on and continue spreading her wonderfulness.

As Serge once said to me, "When the time comes, Joan will go up to Heaven and first ask to see her mother, then her dearly departed family members and friends. Then in her own sweet way she will tell Saint Peter to polish the gates, and then ask to see the gardener." That is Joan—always wanting to be with those she cared about and loved and then wanting to make sure that love and care reflected in everything.

Joan, you will be missed by all, but part of you will always live on in all whose hearts you touched. We love you Joan and may you be in a better place.

* * *

Ken:

Today I want to speak of heroes.

Just recently I was at a funeral for a cousin who was younger than I was but died nevertheless. He was a decorated Vietnam War veteran, a decorated fire chief and volunteer fireman who had rescued people trapped in a burning building.

At his burial, one of my other cousins—there were eight of us who grew up together—started his eulogy with, "Jack was the family hero." And indeed he was, yet the words struck me as a revelation because I had never formed in my mind fully what Jack meant to us. He was, yes, the family's hero.

Well Joan was a hero three times over:

She was hero to her community.

I've lived in Hurleyville 40 years or so and know less than half of the residents in this small town. And I have the feeling half of those don't like me very much. Joan, in contrast, it seems knew everyone and was liked by everyone. I never heard a bad word about her and never heard her speak in an angry fashion about others. Recently, when I would walk into the post office or go out into the street, people would ask, "How's Joanie, how is she doing?"

She was also the hero of the Pizano/Hahn family. She was the liaison between Hurleyville, Minersville, and Florida. Always spoke lovingly about her family; especially her nieces and nephews. Their concerns and tribulations were her concerns.

Once in a group discussion of the family while on a Cultural Events Committee of my temple religious group, the Rabbi said, "It's the wife, the woman who makes the home. She is the one that sets the character of the household, the adhesive that holds it all together. Without her it is a house, not a home." I agree and Joan was the hero of the family home. The walls exuded the personality of Joan. The warmth, friendliness and welcoming tone of the Pizano household that you felt upon walking in reflected the persona of Joan Pizano. She made the house a home.

Joan was also the hero of the Kantor Family. I can recall easily the Christmas table set beautifully (Joan never entertained halfway). I recall—among other events—her calling my kids up the hill to decorate the Christmas tree. In an email letter my daughter sent to Sara while Joan was ailing, my daughter wrote: "I cannot even fathom the emotional roller coaster you are riding. I am very sad in my own way, since your mom has been such a big influence in every stage of my life. Truthfully if not for her, I am not sure my mother would have been able to raise me in one piece. Every bump, splinter and poison ivy episode called for a trip to Joan's house to look at it."

Joan's passing will leave a big void in the Kantor household.

* * *

Then Father Peter asked if anyone else wanted to speak, and five of my mom's friends from the Class of 1957 at The Reading School of Nursing came forward. They told stories of how much they loved Joanie and what a good person she was. Then came the story that made us all gasp!

Apparently, The Joan was encouraging and teaching her nursing school roommate, Marlene, to smoke, and even stuffed towels under the door so they wouldn't get caught in the dorm!!! The room took in a collective and very deep GASP that almost created a black hole!!! However, in all fairness, I do want to remind you that in 1957 doctors were recommending that their patients smoke to improve their health, so The Joan was just part of the conventional wisdom at the time. Anyway, the story remained a topic of conversation for the next two days.

Finally, Isabel (Zizi's twelve-year-old granddaughter, Cat's daughter and Thierry's niece) sat down with her harp. She introduced herself, explained the family connection, and told us that she had asked Aunt Joanie a few months before if she could play the harp for her at The Event. Then she proceeded to play a song that she had written especially for her Aunt Joanie. It was breathtaking and there was not a dry eye in the place.

On Friday morning, we convened at my aunt's house (the funeral home) and then at the church. Father Peter sang and played the violin again ("Ava Maria"), Sister Ana gave the First Reading but only because Morty was late.

(I mention this for a very significant reason. A mere 51 years earlier, that same little Minersville church where my parents were married denied Jewish Morty Goldstein a place at my dad's side as his Best Man. Now, on this day, he was to give the First Reading—only the trip from Brooklyn took longer than expected and he arrived after it was time for the reading. At first, I was upset for my dad but then took his hand as it dawned on me, and I told him, "It's OK, the redemption was in the permission," and I really felt that to be true.)

A Reading from the book of the Prophet Isaiah (as read by Sister Ana):

> On this mountain the Lord of hosts will provide for all peoples
> A feast of rich food and choice wines,
> juicy, rich food and pure, choice wines.
> On this mountain the Lord will destroy the veil that veils all peoples,
> the web that is woven over all nations; He will destroy death forever.
> The Lord God will wipe away the tears from all faces;
> the reproach of his people He will remove from the whole earth;
> for the Most High has spoken. On that day it will be said:
> "Behold our God, to whom we looked to save us!
> This is the Lord for whom we looked;
> let us rejoice and be glad that God has saved us!"
> —The Word of the Lord.

Kevin gave the second reading:

A reading from the Letter of St. Paul to the Romans:

> Brothers and sisters: None of us lives as our own master,
> and none of us dies as our own master.
> For if we live, we live for the Lord,

and if we die, we die for the Lord;
So then, whether we live or die, we belong to the Lord.
For this is why Christ died and came to life,
That He might be Lord of both the dead and the living.
For we shall all stand before the judgment seat of God;
for it is written:
"As I live, says the Lord, every knee shall bend before me,
and every tongue shall give praise to God."
So then each of us shall give an account of ourselves to God.
—The Word of the Lord.

Then the Gospel:

A reading from the Holy Gospel according to John:
Lifting his eyes to heaven, Jesus prayed, saying:
"Holy Father, I do not pray for my disciples alone.
I pray also for those who will believe in me through their word,
that they may be one, as you, Father, are in me, and I in you,
that they may be [one] in us,
so that the world may believe you sent me.

Father, they are your gift to me.
I wish that where I am they also may be with me,
that they may see my glory that you gave me,
because you loved me before the foundation of the world.

Just Father, the world does not know you, but I know you;
and they know that you sent me.
I made your name known to them and I will continue to make it known,
so that your love for me may live in them and I may live in them."
—The Gospel of the Lord (John 17:20-21; 24-26)

Janice and Tip Sukeena delivered the gifts, and during communion Father Peter invited everyone forward. If you didn't want to receive communion, you could get a blessing. After the church we went to the cemetery and laid my mom to rest next to her parents, my precious Nana and Pappy, under blue skies and singing birds.

Over 60 of us finished the celebration at the Blu Tavern where we enjoyed a really good salad, not just lettuce like The Joan had feared. And, you can rest assured that there were <u>no canned peas,</u> and at The Joan's request, there was the most delicious chocolate peanut butter pie and apple cheese pie—the acquisition of which almost killed my cousin Michelle, but that's a whole other chronicle. It wasn't Anne's but filled with the same amount of chocolate and sugar. The fake flowers on the table were my only oversight but a girl can only think of so much!

So for those of you who couldn't join us, I hope that you feel what we all felt last week—an enormous sense of joy and appreciation for my mom in between our tears because we already miss her so much.

So now, my dad, brother and I are working on the painstaking and heartbreaking task of packing and deciding what happens with the contents of the house. We have the appraisal scheduled for this Thursday and the house will go on the market as soon as possible. My dad will be moving to Florida near me in October whether or not the house is sold.

So, for now this is the final chapter of The Joan Chronicles but the beginning of eternity for my mom, so we can rejoice in that—it's just harder for those of us left behind. God bless you all and thank you so much for sending all your love, all the time, to my mom—it meant the world to her and to us.

Much, much love...

Chapter 21

THE APPLE CEREMONY
Just One More
Wednesday, August 8, 2012, 12:51 AM

It wasn't the Final Chapter—I have more, believe it or not. I forgot to tell you about The Apple Ceremony.

The Joan requested that we drop a bag of apples in the back yard for her dear deer after she passed on to Heaven. So last Saturday evening, Serge, Roy, Sue, Ken, Merisa, her friend Melody and her two daughters, Merisa's girls Lexi and Coley, Zizi, Cat, Isabelle, Kevin and I gathered at 107 Main for a cookout. The girls, ages seven-to-twelve, ran around outside like lunatics in their wet bathing suits.

After we ate, we cut the apples into fours, as requested by The Joan, so the deer wouldn't have to work to eat their treats, and hiked into the backyard. Lexi, age nine, videotaped it on her phone, but it was too Blair-Witch-Project to forward to you as she was running and taping simultaneously—nice thought, but it will make you seasick. Coley, of course, asked if she could eat one and I knew The Joan wouldn't want her to be hungry so of course, I said "of course." We threw the apple pieces far and wide and then retired to the deck for our dessert. Dessert was the chocolate peanut butter pie from Anne's that The Joan had wanted for The Event but that we couldn't get because Anne was vacationing (the nerve... after The Joan called Anne to give her a heads-up a few weeks ago!)

Anywho, whilst we ingested a week's worth of calories in one slice of dessert, the girls played a rousing game of Bingo in the sunroom, right

Sara Pizano, MA, DVM

by The Joan's bed. It was the most beautiful thing I have ever seen and a blessing not lost on me. I know my mom was there and so, so happy. And Joanie's Biggest Pearl became crystal clear:

"Live until you breathe your last breath."

Amen.

The Recipes

Nutrition for a person who is ill, especially with a disease that limits their caloric intake, is most essential. During my mom's illness I tried to prepare high protein/high, calorie/nutrition-packed foods. Every bite mattered since very little sustenance was able to get into and through her GI track to be absorbed.

These recipes reflect those needs for my mom but there's also lots of tasty food for a child who is a picky eater, a person debilitated with any illness, or someone recovering from some sort of trauma who needs to gain weight. There are lots of sneaky yet tasty ways to add protein, nutrients and calories to all kinds of menus.

I hope these recipes will inspire you to create your own recipes in an ongoing effort to keep your loved one as healthy as possible. My mom swears the food I made for her gave her the extra months she prayed for.

I always chose full-fat products to add as many calories as possible and compared each label on whatever product I was buying. I was specifically looking for high protein and low sugar items. I was also very careful with salt that could increase my mom's thirst and cause her to retain water. For my mom, protein was the biggest challenge. Carbohydrates are typically easier to blenderize, and added calories so were typically part of each menu.

* * *

MASHED POTATO SHAKE

All ingredients should be added to taste:

Very well cooked and mashed potatoes. For each potato, add:
1 tbsp butter
1 tbsp sour cream
½ inch slice of tofu (use Silkin if you need a thinner shake, firm tofu if you need a thicker shake)
1 scoop protein powder (usually included in the container)
2 tbsp Lactaid

Put all in a blender and blend well, then strain through a super-fine strainer.

* * *

HIGH PROTEIN CREAM OF CHICKEN SOUP

1 whole chicken
10 carrots, peeled and chopped
1 onion, diced
1 head of garlic (diced)
2-3 Idaho potatoes
Olive oil
Butter
1 scoop Protein Powder* per bowl
Half and Half
1 Bay leaf
Pepper

Put the whole chicken in a large pot and cover with water. Then add:

1 head of garlic cut through the middle to expose the garlic
Fresh herbs like rosemary and thyme (handful each)
Salt

Bring the water to a rapid boil then simmer for an hour. The chicken should be cooked and tender. Legs/wings should be easy to remove at this point but if not, cook longer until chicken is done. When done, remove chicken from pot and after the chicken has cooled, remove the skin and meat. Remember to use all the meat, as the dark meat has more fat, and is good for a debilitated person who needs to gain weight or eat more calories. Pour liquid from the pot through a strainer and use as the stock for the soup.

In a separate pot, boil the potatoes until mushy and mash with butter and Half and Half. Set aside.

Next, sauté the carrots, one clove of garlic, and diced onion until all are soft. For a debilitated person, you cannot cook them too much as you want them as soft as possible, just don't burn them.

In a blender mix the chicken stock, shredded chicken, protein powder, carrot mixture, mashed potato mixture, salt and pepper to taste

If too thick, stir in more Half and Half to add more calories. If too thin, add more chicken or mashed potatoes. My mom liked to eat things with different consistencies or textures, as much as she could. She liked the variety.

*There are a variety of Protein Powders available, so read labels carefully. In my mom's case I wanted a lot of protein but low fiber, since her intestines could not process the fiber. I also wanted to avoid sugar because each bite needed to be packed with only nutritious ingredients. Sugary foods can be digested quickly, spike your blood sugar then drop it fast so you feel hungry sooner. I wanted her to feel satisfied for the longest period of time since only a percentage of what she was eating was actually getting into her intestines.

* * *

PEAR FRANGIPANE

I found this recipe in Parade magazine while I was staying in the Catskill Mountains in upstate New York. It's my go-to dessert to make a great impression on guests, and my mom loved it.

PASTRY
1 cup flour
¼ tsp salt
6 tbsp cold, unsalted butter, cut into small pieces
2 tbsp ice water

Put flour and salt in a food processor and pulse to blend. Add butter and pulse until mixture resembles coarse cornmeal. Add ice water and pulse until the mixture sticks together. Mold into a ball, cover in plastic wrap and refrigerate for an hour.

Roll out dough and place in a 9-inch tart pan with removable bottom. Press pastry onto the sides of the pan and trim top. Bake for 20 minutes then let cool.

FRANGIPANE
6 tbsp butter
²/₃ cup sugar
¾ cup ground almonds
2 tsp sifted flour
1 tsp cornstarch
1 egg
1 egg white
1 tsp vanilla extract
1 tsp almond extract
3 soft, ripe pears, peeled and cut into halves lengthwise and cored

Place butter and sugar into the bowl of the food processor and process until smooth. Add almonds and blend then add flour, cornstarch, egg and egg white. Process until smooth, then add vanilla and almond extract and blend well.

Spread frangipane in pastry tart then arrange pears overlapping in a star configuration and nestle into mixture.

Bake at 375 degrees for 40 minutes until frangipane is puffy and golden. Delicious!

* * *

CHICKEN MEATBALLS WITH PEANUT SAUCE

My mom couldn't eat this whole meal but wanted it included in "The Joan Chronicles." I did, however, strain the peanut sauce and put it over a variety of things she could eat and she loved it.

Mix together:

1 lb. ground chicken (I recommend getting the package that says "ground chicken" and not "ground chicken breast," since I really feel the fat added moisture to the meatball disguised as dark meat)
½ cup finely diced onion
½ finely diced red pepper
½ cup finely diced fresh cilantro
1 egg
½ tsp salt
1 tsp fresh grated ginger
½ cup plain breadcrumbs
1 tbsp olive oil

Form into meatballs and sauté in the olive oil on all sides over medium heat, about 5-6 minutes then remove from pan.
In same pan (after you remove the meatballs) mix together:

1 cup coconut milk
½ cup chicken broth
2 tbsp low salt soy sauce
½ tsp fresh grated ginger
½ cup reduced fat peanut butter

Stir constantly over medium heat to melt the peanut butter. Bring to a simmer (I have no idea what that means—I'm just the messenger) and cook 2-3 minutes until slightly thickened. Add meatballs to sauce, cover pan and cook 5 minutes or until meatballs are cooked through. This dish goes well with basmati rice and 13% Food TV Network approved Pinot Grigio.

* * *

DARK CHOCOLATE MOUSSE
(But I would call it "Serious Chocolate Pudding" instead)

12.3 ounce package of Silken tofu, drained (this is why I liked this recipe for The Joan but I also think it's good for kids who like chocolate as it's an easy way to sneak in protein and, I pinky swear to all of you tofu haters, that you will never know it's in there!)
3 ozs bittersweet chocolate, finely chopped
¼ cup unsweetened cocoa powder
¼ cup water
1 tbsp brandy (we didn't have any brandy in the house and I voted *"no" on adding Yuengling, so The Joan said to add her favorite Christmastime liquor—Harvey's Bristol Cream)*
½ cup sugar

Puree the tofu until smooth (this is a really important step because if you don't there are little unsightly white specs in the mousse). Put the chopped chocolate, cocoa powder, ¼ cup water and brandy in a saucepan or heat-proof bowl fitted over a pot containing one inch barely simmering water. Stir frequently until melted and smooth, then remove from heat. Mix in the sugar a little at a time until smooth. Add the chocolate mixture with the tofu and puree until smooth. Cover and refrigerate at least an hour.

Disclaimer: The above recipe came out more like a super chocolate, chocolate pudding instead of mousse, so if that's your thing, you can stop there. At 107 Main, we did a taste test and the above recipe became Recipe "A."

Then I did the following to create Recipe "B": Whip ½ pint of heavy cream until almost stiff (and way before it turns to butter) then add 1 tsp of sugar and ½ tsp of super great quality vanilla and whip until it peaks.

* * *

SANIYE'S VEGAN EGGPLANT PARM

1 large eggplant, washed and cut into 1-inch cubes
1 chopped medium onion
1 package soft or medium tofu, mashed with a fork
6 tbsp nutritional yeast
Olive oil
5 sliced fresh tomatoes
2 cloves of chopped garlic
Fresh herbs of your choosing
1 tablespoon chopped basil
Sea salt to taste

Toss the eggplant with a little olive oil and sea salt and roast in the oven at 425 degrees for 20-25 minutes, flipping half way through the cook time.

Sauté the onion and garlic in small amount of olive oil until slightly soft, then add the mashed tofu and nutritional yeast. Sauté for 5-10 minutes with a little sea salt.

In a square baking dish, layer the tomatoes (or sauce), eggplant, and tofu mixture. Top with slices of fresh tomatoes and chopped basil.

Bake for 45 minutes at 350 degrees. Let sit for 15 minutes before serving.

* * *

COUSIN MICHELLE'S FABULOUS CHEESECAKE

CRUST

1¾ cup graham crackers
¼ cup chopped walnuts
½ tsp cinnamon
½ cup melted butter

Cream together:
2 (8oz) cream cheese (softened)
1 cup sugar

Sara Pizano, MA, DVM

Blend in:
   3 well beaten eggs
   ¼ tsp salt
   1 tsp vanilla extract
   1 tsp almond extract

Add and mix until uniform:
   3 cups sour cream

Bake in springform pan at 375 degrees for 35 minutes or until set, then top with strawberries and glaze, pie filling or fresh fruit.

*To add more protein, add 1 scoop protein powder and a ½ inch slice of Silken tofu.

107 Main

Printed in the United States
By Bookmasters